For Gwen Macleod

— our mam,

and a great trade unionist and socialist

GETTING BY

Estates, class and culture in austerity Britain

Lisa Mckenzie

First published in Great Britain in 2015 by

Policy Press
University of Bristol
1-9 Old Park Hill
Bristol
BS2 8BB
UK
t: +44 (0)117 954 5940
pp-info@bristol.ac.uk
www.policypress.co.uk

North America office:
Policy Press
c/o The University of Chicago Press
1427 East 60th Street
Chicago, IL 60637, USA
t: +1 773 702 7700
f: +1 773 702 9756
sales@press.uchicago.edu
www.press.uchicago.edu

© Policy Press 2015
Reprinted 2017

British Library Cataloguing in Publication Data
A catalogue record for this book is available from the British Library

Library of Congress Cataloging-in-Publication Data
A catalog record for this book has been requested

ISBN 978 1 44730 995 6 paperback
ISBN 978 1 44731 129 4 ePub
ISBN 978 1 44731 130 0 Kindle

The right of Lisa Mckenzie to be identified as author of this work has been asserted by her in accordance with the Copyright, Designs and Patents Act.1988

The statements and opinions contained within this publication are solely those of the author and not of the University of Bristol or Policy Press. The University of Bristol and Policy Press disclaim responsibility for any injury to persons or property resulting from any material published in this publication.

Policy Press works to counter discrimination on grounds of gender, race, disability, age and sexuality.

Cover design by Soapbox, www.soapbox.co.uk
Printed and bound in Great Britain by CMP, Poole
Policy Press uses environmentally responsible print partners

Contents

Acknowledgements

Low-income working class families have over the last two generations been increasingly positioned to rely on the state to ensure they have enough to survive. This is because of low wages, or no wages, the precarity of the financial markets and because of the inadequate and shameful state of social housing in the United Kingdom. These families, and communities deserve respect, dignity, pride and acknowledgment. Consequently I would like to acknowledge all of those in the UK who are finding themselves in this increasingly precarious position. I hope I am able to do you justice within this book, and I promise I will never give up the fight against inequality, and the lack of justice in our society for working-class people and communities.

Thank you to my family from the Carsic Estate in Sutton-in-Ashfield for instilling in me at a very young age a class pride and a determination to know that 'we' are people of value, we are strong, and our communities are important to us above all else. These values are the greatest gift anyone could be given, and they are my inheritance from my long line of Derbyshire farmhands and Nottinghamshire miners. Margaret Thatcher, her boys and their ideology did not break these despite the war they waged on us in 1984. We did not lose those.

I need to thank the community in St Ann's for adopting me as their own when I was a young 19-year-old mother and needed help. I have had the most happiness and a lot of sadness on this estate so thank you for your continued help and support over 25 years. I hope I have done your kindness, hardships, spirit and humour justice.

My colleagues in the academic world have supported me and believed in me when I really didn't believe in myself especially John Holmwood and Gurminder Bhambra, Bev Skeggs and, more recently, Mike Savage. Thank you, I hope I have proved worth it.

Alison Shaw at Policy Press who from the day she met me has supported this project and believed in it. This book would really not have happened without her. I am eternally grateful for her support.

To the late Ken Coates and to Bill Silburn all I can say to you is my admiration and respect for lives lived fighting inequality is endless. You are both giants and they truly don't make them like you anymore.

Lastly I could not have written this book without the support and love from my dad, Ian Macleod, who I cannot say how proud of him I am. One of only 15 miners who stayed out at SilverHill Pit in 1984.

And to my son, Leon, who is always the light in any dark time.

Note: Throughout my research all names have been changed, to offer anonymity to the individual residents who have spoken to me and become part of this narrative from St Ann's.

About the author

Lisa Mckenzie left school officially in May 1984 when she was 16 years old. Unofficially she left in early March that year because of the disruption the police were causing when they invaded the small mining town in Nottinghamshire where she lived with her striking family. She worked at the Pretty Polly factory making tights until she was 25, then worked part time in shops in Nottingham city centre before working in housing projects and homeless hostels. She enrolled on an Access course in 2000, eventually completing her higher education at the University of Nottingham following an undergraduate degree, a master's degree and finally handing in her PhD in September 2009.

She has used her experience in and out of university to collect stories, and to interpret the narratives from people she cares passionately about because of the levels of injustice visited on them. She considers her research to be active and political sociology, and herself as an activist sociologist.

Foreword

The world is changing rapidly. A century ago almost all accounts of the lives of the poor were written by the rich and often for the rich. Occasional exceptions, such as *The ragged trousered philanthropists* (Tressell, 1914), proved the rule. Lisa Mckenzie begins her account of life in St Ann's with her reaction to reading George Orwell's observation that the poor smelt.

Fifty years ago social observation had become the territory of the concerned middle class and other only slightly less affluent outsiders. In this book Lisa talks more warmly of Ken Coates' and Richard Silburn's studies of St Ann's, published as *Poverty: The forgotten Englishmen* by Penguin in 1970. But these were still outsiders' perspectives, shocking the English middle class of the day by revealing that areas remained in England where not all children had shoes. Ken had been a Nottinghamshire miner, but only came to that because he refused to be conscripted into the army.

Today those who have been poor increasingly write their own stories of living in poverty. Lisa's family were Derbyshire agricultural labourers and Nottinghamshire miners with few other employment opportunities. From leaving school around the age of 15 she worked at the Pretty Polly factory making tights until she was 25, then worked part time in shops in Nottingham city centre. She has been homeless, and afraid. She did too much too young. She had a mixed-race child and lived in St Ann's as a young mother.

Lisa later spent many years at Nottingham University becoming a social scientist – learning how to use long words, to anonymise the identities of her interviewees, to call people by their surnames when writing, to read obscure texts, to produce a PhD thesis and to get funding to study the estate she lived on – but she didn't have to struggle to know what she was talking about. She only had to struggle to learn how to talk about it in the ways expected for a largely middle-class, academic readership.

Today we translate. We describe the different worlds we live in to each other as those worlds move apart. More and more people try to span these worlds. Observation is not longer enough; immersion is no longer enough. As the gaps between our experiences grow it becomes ever more necessary to hear largely first-hand, unadulterated accounts, the descriptions from the inside.

In *On the run: Fugitive life in an American city*, Alice Goffman (2014) recently told of her experiences of living for six years in one of the poorest quarters of the US – that is the US equivalent of this UK book, but Lisa gets nearer to the bone.

Lisa also works from the inside, but with the greater insight because she is that much closer to those she is reporting on. There is much less surprise expressed in this book at the state of things, and much more surprise about how little many academics and the rest of the affluent (or mildly affluent) understand the world they share. Lisa's recent immersion has been in the university; she has always been in the city.

The very different roles of women and men are clear in both Mckenzie's and Goffman's work. Goffman's America is more violent; prison is much more usual for men, while eviction is the common and comparable experience for women. Even in the poorest parts of Nottingham it is still not the norm for the majority of men to have been in prison or so many relatively young women to have faced the bailiffs and been put out on the street with their children. But the poorest areas of Nottingham are now moving in the direction of Detroit and Los Angeles.

There are other connections between life in the poorest parts of the US, the most economically unequal of all large rich nations, and the UK, the most economically unequal in Europe. For example, men in the poorest parts of Nottingham subscribe to conspiracy theories more and more readily to explain why they are where they are (p 96). Often UK-recycled conspiracy theories come from the poorer parts of the US, from where the YouTube videos are posted, suggesting that 'the Illuminati apparently infiltrate and control American hip-hop music' (p 97). Lisa recounts '…elaborate theories that relate to the American hip-hop artist and rapper Jay-Z, and his wife and pop star diva Beyoncé who, they believe, are puppets for the Zionists' (p 97). These theories cross the Atlantic just as easily as the 747s that daily carry so many bankers between London and New York, one every two minutes at peak times.

Getting by continues a tradition of reporting on the poorest areas, but it also continues the tradition of updating how that is done and by whom. It has only taken one hundred years to move from well-meaning upper-class men writing these accounts, to today having them written by more knowledgeable working-class women. One hundred years may seem a very long time but it is a revolution. Not only are the class divides growing but more and more people are trying to leap over those divides to explain one rapidly changing world to another rapidly changing world.

Lisa describes some of the names now given to babies in the neighbourhood: Shanelle, Dior, Tyree and Ymani. Contrast them with the names the extremely rich Candy brothers gave their children at a similar time: Isabella Monaco Evanthia and Cayman Charles Wolf.

The Candy brothers, Nick and Christian, are not that differently named from any Lisa or Danny, or George, Alice and Ken – but forenames in future will be much more of a class give-away than in the recent past. We (in the upper middle) tend to ridicule the names of those at the bottom and the top, without realising just how odd apparently 'normal' names may soon become.

We are dividing. Just as upper-class people increasingly live in upper-class ghettos, sending their children to upper-class schools – not just to give them a huge head-start but to try to escape the class prejudice that very posh kids might experience in the average state school – so too some of the lowest-class people stay in St Ann's because it provides 'safety from class prejudice' as Lisa puts it. The rich and poor stay in places you might have thought they would try harder to leave, despite the cost for both groups.

For the upper classes, their schools and houses cost a fortune. They may feel they have to send their children to boarding school, because it is the done thing. For the lower classes, the cost of the stigma of living in the poorest area – of not being offered jobs because of your postcode, and the cost to your children's life chances of not getting out if you can get out – is also partly outweighed because leaving is not the done thing. How would you fit in elsewhere? It is not the done thing to trust others who are not like you, and this applies whether you are very rich or very poor.

Lisa ends her story by explaining how the police still fit people up and what results when that happens. The police stand between rich and poor. They keep order, not just in the literal sense of apparently preventing trouble by being about, but the social order between the haves and have-nots.

For much of my life I thought we were moving away from the racism and police violence I saw as child. We may have, a bit, but I have also been getting more posh. And much now is getting worse. It's not just the cuts and the food banks. It's also the attitude, including the attitude of authority. Or as Lisa puts it,

> I realise that Britain is a far more dangerous place for our children than it was prior to the shooting of Mark Duggan. The fear of the young black, or mixed-race, man, and the loathing for the families who live on council estates, have been institutionalised and legitimated through the courts and our legal system. (p 192)

People are getting by, but it's getting much worse at the bottom, and you are unlikely to know the half of it because that is the way it currently is. Britain is once again as economically unequal as it was when Orwell was writing in the 1930s. The best-off 1 per cent once again take 15 per cent of all income.[1] In the years in between we came together and then fell apart – we came together before, when we began to recognise just how bad the repercussions of falling apart really are. There are worse things than just 'getting by' and we are currently heading towards them.

Danny Dorling
Oxford, October 2014

[1] Dorling, D. (2014) *Inequality and the 1%*, London: Verso Books.

Introduction

The importance of narrative

George Orwell asked, in *The road to Wigan Pier* (1962), 'do the "lower classes" smell?' He answered this immediately with 'Of course, as a whole, they are dirtier than the upper classes.' He goes on to say that, given the circumstances of their living and working conditions, their lack of resources, time and money, they were bound to be dirtier than those with more resources. Orwell raises this question in response to his revelation that as a member of the upper middle class he was taught that the lower classes were inferior and that they smelt, and he noted that this lesson had stayed with him throughout his life.

I first read *The road to Wigan Pier* as a 16-year-old. I was given a copy by an editor, Annie Pike, from Penguin Books, who visited my family home in North Nottinghamshire during the miners' strike in 1984. We were a striking family and frequently had visitors from odd places offering support. Annie came up from London once a month with a cheque for about £20, funds she had raised in her office to support miners' families. My mother was chair of Women Against Pit Closures Teversal and Silver Hill Branch, and I had just left school and started work at the Pretty Polly factory making tights with my mother and aunties. On one of these visits Annie talked to me about George Orwell, after a conversation I had had with her about my love of reading. She brought me a collection of books by Barry Hines and George Orwell. I still have those books, although I have not seen Annie since 1984.

Reading George Orwell as a 16-year-old working-class girl living in a mining community during the 1984 miners' strike was difficult. I didn't pick that book up again until 2001 when I went to university. Orwell's depiction of working-class life during the 1930s was upsetting; this was the time of my grandparents who had raised me until I was six years old, and whom I dearly loved. The knowledge that 'others' had been taught that they smelt and were dirty was very painful, and led me to think about how we were known and thought of in 1984. I had not considered this at all in my 16 years. I was the daughter, granddaughter, and niece of miners. I knew I was working class, and I had been taught that we were the backbone of the country, strong and proud, and it never occurred to me that 'others' did not think the same. During 1984 and 1985 I learned that outside of my mining community, and outside of the working class, those old prejudices were alive and well, and instead of being the backbone of Britain, we became 'the enemy within'. Working-class communities in the UK have been destroyed since 1985. Am I being sentimental, or over-dramatic? Perhaps, but destroyed is what I see, and destroyed is what I feel now, living on an inner-city council estate in Nottingham.

Reading *The road to Wigan Pier* has always been painful. I think of my mother, and grandmother, obsessively washing net curtains, with the mantra 'we might be poor but we are not dotty [dirty]'. Did they know how we were seen through the eyes of the middle class? I think they did, and the testimonies in this book show that others still do. Orwell says that as a middle-class child he was trained to wash his neck, die for his country, and despise the lower classes. As a working-class woman who now works in a university surrounded by the middle class, I think that middle-class children are trained to think they have a right to a higher education. I think dying for their country is off the list, and I am unsure about washing their necks, but I would wager that despising the lower classes is still on the list.

Orwell argues that how one class sees another is vitally important if we are to understand and, eventually, rid ourselves of class distinction. It is painful to think that you are not good enough, or to think yourself a failure, no matter what the context – when it is a whole class of people who have been known over generations as failures, not good enough and distasteful, there are severe consequences of being the butt of ingrained class prejudice, inequality and stigmatisation.

It is often assumed that working-class life is one-dimensional and easily comprehended. Working-class people's practices, what they do, are consequently misinterpreted and misunderstood by those who are trying to understand something they know little about. Reading the words of George Orwell again from the outside I am defensive, and I am hurt; however, on the inside I am also laughing. Do the working class really smell?

I think about my own childhood growing up in that mining town – Sunday night was bath night, which included washing our hair, every Sunday, if we wanted it or not. I remember negotiating with my mother and grandmother about this weekly activity. It was never anything we looked forward to, and we especially hated the hair washing. I never realised until I was an adult that other children had baths much more frequently than once a week. On my estate, once a week was average, and some children got away with less. Hence, like many of the stories within this book, this one about my Sunday night bath time appears easy to follow, as by my own admission I am suggesting Orwell's perception of the working class might be right. However, like all narratives, there is a context to this one, and a backstory.

We lived in a three-bedroomed brick council house built after the First World War. It had one coal fire in the living room, which was supposed to heat the house and the water. It was, in fact, inadequate for the size of the house and for the seven people who lived in it. The house was cold, and there was damp in the bedrooms, and hot water was limited. So baths were also limited, and we hated them.

My sister and I would run downstairs in towels, shivering and sitting on the hearth to get warm again. We hated having our hair washed. We used washing-up liquid, which made our heads and skin itch, and got into our eyes. Oh how I coveted 'Matey', a branded bubble bath that was advertised on television during the early 1970s and aimed at small children. It had a catchy tune, and the bottle was shaped like a sailor. I desperately wanted a bottle of 'Matey' for our Sunday night bath; unfortunately, my mother thought bubble bath for children was too frivolous for our house, so bath time continued with washing-up liquid. The once-a-week baths were adequate for our environment, we were well presented at school, and we didn't smell. However, I imagine our cleanliness may not have been to the same standard as those who lived in centrally heated housing, and who could afford an emersion heater, proper shampoo, and whose mother didn't fall into fits of laughter when her daughter suggested buying 'special bubble bath for children'.

This book is filled with stories like my own – fortunately not all of my own, but stories and narratives I have collected over the last nine years from the St Ann's estate in Nottingham. My own social position is important to the research that I undertake, but also to this account of council estate life. My stories link me with the people who are represented in this book – I would not have been allowed to collect them and represent them here without my relationships with these people, and the mutual respect and knowledge that I have built up over many years. Academic researchers have often been accused of being distant, or only speaking to each other – this book is none of those things. It is a story from the inside, but also one that aims to challenge the simplistic and uncomplicated way that council estate life is often represented. This constant tug of war between concepts of 'inside' and 'outside' is a key theme throughout this book – what happens 'inside' the estate in relation to 'outside', whether you are known on the estate as an 'insider' or an 'outsider', and what those on the 'outside' think about those on the 'inside' feature heavily throughout.

My own journey into higher education, and into university life, is also important. The University of Nottingham is only three miles away from St Ann's council estate, where I live. Until I attended an

interview I had never even been to the university – residents of
St Ann's know very little about this great institution for learning,
which is on their doorstep. Although the route from St Ann's to the
University of Nottingham is 20 minutes by bus, symbolically, it is
further away than China (where the university also has a campus).

After my mother died in 1999 I enrolled on an Access course
at a local college. Like most working-class women I wanted to do
something more worthwhile with my life – I thought I could do
more than make tights in a factory, or stand for hours on end bored
in a shop. I wanted to work in my community, to give something
back, and, like most working-class people entering education, I could
not take a risk on 'education for education's sake'. I needed to know
I was doing something that I could get a job with. I intended to go
on to higher education and to train as a social worker. I had known
another woman who had done this.

While studying at college we had a visit from a lecturer from
the School of Sociology and Social Policy at the University of
Nottingham. He introduced us to a study, *Poverty: The forgotten
Englishmen* (1970). This had been undertaken by researchers at the
University of Nottingham, Ken Coates and Bill Silburn, showing
how poverty was still a serious problem in Nottingham during the
1960s. The research was set in St Ann's, and concluded that people
who lived there were suffering terrible hardships because of poor
housing, and low wages. I didn't know that this was a subject that you
could study at university, or that communities like St Ann's, where
I lived, were interesting and relevant to academic studies. I changed
direction at that point and applied to the School of Sociology and
Social Policy at the University of Nottingham. After reading that
study, I always intended to tell my own story of council estate life.
After my undergraduate degree I secured funding for four years' post-
graduate study, and to research St Ann's, initially focusing on mothers
living in the neighbourhood. After finishing my PhD in 2010 I won
a Leverhulme Fellowship to continue the research in St Ann's, this
time focusing on the men in the estate. This book is the outcome
of nine years' academic research; it is the fruits of that labour, and
the fruition of my goal, to tell my own story of council estate life.

Narratives, and storytelling, are important in working-class lives. It is how we explain ourselves, how we understand the world around us, and how we situate ourselves in a wider context. We learn to make sense of what sometimes seems senseless through narratives. Anyone who has done qualitative research will know it is very difficult to get a succinct answer from a working-class respondent. It is much easier and more interesting to listen to 'their story' from the very beginning, and to see where it goes. My research and this book are focused on St Ann's housing estate in Nottingham from 2005 until 2013. The book spans New Labour's explanation of inequality through the use of 'social exclusion', up to the Cameron revelation that 'Britain is broken', and we can all guess who broke it: the bankers? Politicians? No, of course not. It was the poor working class and welfare-dependent that spoilt it for everyone (according to the Conservative Party). Although the experiences and the narratives in this book may be difficult to understand if you have never lived your life in the abyss of the 'underclass', or feared becoming the reviled 'undeserving poor' by being made redundant from your job, both these terms are used to describe the poorest 10 per cent of the population. The aims of this book are clear, that inequality in the UK is increasing, and the consequences of those living within the poorest neighbourhoods are severe, frightening to them and long-lasting in their effects. The poorest 10 per cent of the population in the UK are becoming further away from 'the rest', working in extremely low-paid employment, most relying on various state welfare benefits, and their lives are precarious.

The focus of this research and this book is, therefore, the council housing estate in Nottingham and council estate life, the inequalities and disadvantages that those who live on the estate both perceive and directly experience. However, the dimensions of those inequalities, through gender, class, race and ethnicity, are also important; 'class and welfare' are important features, but I also argue that although there is an economic dimension to inequality (what you have, what you earn, how and what you are entitled to), there is also a cultural dimension that feeds into stigma (what you wear, how you speak, your accent, your tastes). The residents who live on this estate know only too well how difficult it is to live with unfair representations of 'who you are' and of how you live your life, and the serious and negative impacts those representations can have. They know that they are looked down on, that they are represented as not good enough, and that their tastes are often rubbished or ridiculed. This is hurtful but also has a negative effect on your life chances, your opportunities. You become stigmatised.

Representations and value

I first started to think about representations of working-class people in a critical way during my undergraduate studies at the University of Nottingham – as I have said, I became aware of how 'others' saw my community and family in a damaging way during the 1980s when to be 'working class' in the UK seemed to be old fashioned, silly, and backward. However, it was while at university as a mature student many years later that I started to understand how damaging these types of negative representations are to working-class people. As an undergraduate, I was introduced to the work of Pierre Bourdieu, a French social theorist, sociologist, and ethnographer; I found his words difficult to understand, and written in complex ways that I thought I would never grasp. At the same time I was introduced to the work of another sociologist, Bev Skeggs (1997). I later found out she was also from a working-class background, and her words, and work, really resonated with me. I read her first book, *Formations of class and gender*, an ethnographic account of young working-class women on a caring course in the North East of England, and I began to think about how working-class women in particular were represented in very negative ways. Bev Skeggs' research drew on the theoretical work of Pierre Bourdieu. She used his framework of 'capital', which helped me understand how some groups in society are subject to become 'misrecognised', and how they can become devalued. It was her work that helped me to understand the work of Pierre Bourdieu – she used his theoretical tools in explaining class inequality through respect, and recognition.

Class injustice: disrespect, misrecognition and non-recognition

What I consequently learned through the work of Bev Skeggs, and other mostly female scholars such as Diane Reay, Imogen Tyler and Stephanie Lawler, was that legitimation is key to understanding how some are valued as others are devalued. What happens is that something becomes of value through becoming legitimate, and conversely, practices, resources and people can also become illegitimate. 'Misrecognition' is a term we use in sociology to understand the classification of the legitimate and the illegitimate, and what Pierre Bourdieu and Loïc Wacquant call the function of 'symbolic violence', which they define as 'the violence which is exercised upon a social agent with his or her complicity' (1992, p167). In other words, according to Bourdieu and Wacquant, people are subjected to forms of violence, which can include being treated as inferior and denied resources, and they are limited in their social mobility and aspirations. However, these people do not perceive it in that way. Rather, their situation seems to them to be 'the natural order of things'. Another scholar, Nancy Fraser, argues that 'symbolic violence' through misrecognition is a class injustice that can be cultural or symbolic, and is rooted in social patterns of representation, interpretation, and communication (Fraser, 1997).

Bev Skeggs' work in Manchester illustrates a type of cultural and class injustice, as some of the women in her study go through life trying to accumulate middle-class culture as their only means of improving their working-class positions. This type of injustice is central within the politics of aspiration, when sections of society are being forced to dis-identify with their 'working classness', their culture, in order to 'self-improve'. The women in Skeggs' study try to adopt middle-class culture through ways of dressing and speaking. However, they are always aware that they can never 'do middle class right' (Skeggs, 1997, p 82). They are aware that they get it wrong, and they do not feel comfortable when they enter the space inhabited by the middle class; they therefore feel 'shame' about their social position (Skeggs, 1997, p 88).

In addition to cultural misrecognition there is also non-recognition, when those who are devalued can be rendered invisible, and this becomes especially relevant when examining class inequality within gender. Returning to the women in Skeggs' study, they often complained about 'feeling invisible', especially when they went shopping in Manchester, and in particular in the upmarket department stores. The women noted that when they visited these stores, they were never sprayed with perfume as they noticed 'other' women were. They complained to Skeggs that they 'weren't scruffy or doing anything wrong'; however, they knew they were being judged only on their class position, therefore being denied the 'norms' of the perfume department, a 'middle-class space' where they did not belong.

There is another position of class injustice that is linked to disrespect, and how those who are deemed as valueless are disrespected for being 'themselves'. Pierre Bourdieu argues throughout his work that space is extremely important when looking at a cultural or symbolic injustice of class, as these injustices are only apparent in certain spaces, mainly 'middle-class space', or space where working-class culture is not legitimate, tolerated, and needs moderating. Consequently, the way that space is occupied means that some have a more 'legitimate' entitlement to both social and cultural space than others. Those people who are misrecognised, non-recognised or disrespected because of 'who' they are rather than what they may or may not have done are acts of symbolic violence.

'Broken' Britain

Symbolic violence has been visited on the poor for many generations in the UK, often through the language of the 'underclass' and the negative connotations attributed to those that it describes. The language, which demeans the poor, is powerful and has been with us for many generations, and political parties both left and right have used it in gaining political capital among the electorate, when needed. Margaret Thatcher, in the 1980s, along with Charles Murray, who later became the co-author of the notorious *Bell curve* (Herrnstein and Murray, 1994), spoke clearly of the problems the 'underclass' caused with their 'cycle of poverty', while the Blair government used the language of exclusion and 'the excluded' (Welshman, 2007, pp 4-6). The Cameron Conservatives commissioned a report by the right-wing think tank, the Centre for Social Justice, in 2006 to look at welfare in the UK. They came back with the *Breakdown Britain* report, and have used the relative successful concept of 'the broken' to explain inequality as a product of family breakdown. Hence families are broken, values are broken, communities are broken, children are broken, our schools, welfare and healthcare systems are also broken, and consequently, Britain is broken (Slater, 2012).

Since 2010 the Conservative Party and the Liberal Democrat Coalition government have introduced severe and punitive measures, relating to their austerity programme designed to mend Britain's 'broken' finances. This was after the banking crash in 2008. However, by 2010, and certainly by 2014, the focus moved from bankers to welfare claimants and public sector workers. Draconian measures have been introduced to the welfare system in all areas – Unemployment Benefit, disability benefits, Income Support and Housing Benefit in particular. In just over three years, communities, and people who were already living very precarious lives before 2010, have had many services and benefits cut. This has left families and communities in dire situations, where people have to choose whether to heat their homes or to eat. Parents have to choose which child needs a new pair of shoes the most at the beginning of the school year. Unemployment within these neighbourhoods, particularly among young people and minority ethnic groups, is becoming desperate.

There has also been civil unrest during these few short years. In August 2011, what has been called the 'England riots' hit many inner-city neighbourhoods throughout the UK, following the shooting and death of a young man in Tottenham, London, by the police. Prime Minister David Cameron, during that week of civil unrest, again spoke about 'the broken society', and promised the outraged British public that tackling 'broken families, and broken communities' was at the top of his list. The Conservative's report *Breakdown Britain* identified 120,000 'troubled families', and after the 2011 riots Mr Cameron said he would speed up plans to improve their parenting skills, to 'fix' broken Britain. Part of the 'broken' Britain rhetoric has been the 'moral collapse' within the inner city, and Cameron also pledged a war on gang affiliation within inner-city communities.

The over-arching rhetoric of 'broken' Britain is family breakdown, which, the Centre for Social Justice says, 'is directly related to the rise in thuggary, drug abuse and street violence' (CSJ, 2006). It was reported in *The Telegraph* that 'the number of young people stabbed to death in the past three years suggests a street life reminiscent of William Golding's *Lord of the flies*' (Kendall, 2009). The Conservatives' 'broken' Britain thesis focuses on the premise that there is an underclass, which has a disproportionate influence in terms of the 'crime it spawns' and the 'huge amount of public money it soaks up – mostly in welfare benefits and funding for the criminal justice system.'

The government's own figures in 2010 estimated there were one million more people living in 'severe poverty' (defined as earning 40 per cent of the average national wage) than in 1997 (CSJ, 2006). This has risen significantly since the austerity measures started to have an impact on communities after the 2010 General Election. In 2013 the Institute for Fiscal Studies (IFS) published a report revealing that in the first full year of the coalition government, 300,000 more children faced a real fall in living standards that had pushed them into dire levels of poverty (Cribb et al, 2013). The entire increase is from homes where parents are working – there are now 2.4 million children in working households living in severe poverty. And on top of the 300,000 extra young people living below the breadline, half-a-million working-age adults have fallen into the extreme poverty bracket, along with an additional 100,000 pensioners (Cribb et al, 2013).

The *Breakdown Britain* report, which has been the source and justification for many of the welfare changes implemented by Iain Duncan-Smith, Conservative Party Secretary of State for Work and Pensions, identifies 'five poverty drivers': family breakdown; welfare dependency; educational failure; addiction to drugs and alcohol; and serious personal debt. All of this squarely puts the problems of society on the individual. According to the 'broken' Britain thesis, it is personal failure and 'bad behaviour' that has broken Britain.

The myths of the 'benefit scrounger'

With the recent and damaging rhetoric presented by politicians through the Conservatives' 'broken' narrative, and previously with New Labour's 'exclusion' meaning the poorest were excluding themselves through their 'bad behaviour' (Welshman, 2007, pp 193-6), over the last four years the media have made much capital by writing about and screening what has been known as 'poverty porn' – the prurient fascination of just how badly behaved the poor have become, with the particular lens focused on those claiming state benefits with aptly titled programmes such as 'We pay your benefits', and the now notorious 'Benefits Street'. Tracy Jensen, from the University of East London, wrote in a recent comment piece that there is a clear symbolic division between 'worker' and 'shirker', or, in the current manifestation, 'skiver' and 'striver', embedded in the narrative of recent media and political rhetoric of Britain's working-class population (Jensen, 2013). It has become popular opinion, and almost the default understanding, that those who live on council housing estates in the UK are overly dependent on welfare and state benefits, because of their own 'lifestyle choices', using taxpayers' hard-earned money seemingly to live the life of 'Riley', which often includes taking drugs, drinking alcohol and generally having a great time, if we are to believe the 'poverty porn' narrative. However, recent research from Shildrick et al (2012, pp 220-3). provides clear evidence that this view of the lives of those who live on council estates and the working-class poor is false. They describe the cycle of their lives as a 'longitudinal pattern of employment instability and movement between low-paid jobs and employment, usually accompanied by claiming of welfare benefits' (Shildrick et al, 2012, p 18)". Far from being 'lazy' or 'work-shy', many people claiming unemployment benefits do so over short spells, in between periods of low-paid, poor-quality, precarious, short-term or zero-hours work. And this kind of work is increasing in neoliberal Britain at a faster rate than permanent, full-time, living wage work. Importantly, low-pay low-skill work is no longer confined to entry-level work, which has been seen in the past as a stepping-stone into better paid and more stable employment, but constitutes a 'sticky state' of work, a cycle of entrapment which has a powerful stigmatising effect in terms of future opportunities.

The clear message from this extended and rigorous research from the North East of England is that unemployment has never been a lifestyle choice; neither has claiming benefits for an extended period of time. Unemployment and benefit claiming has always meant a life of poverty, insecurity, and precarity. Low pay, no pay, zero-hours contracts, and low-grade self-employed work have left families in extremely precarious positions in recent years; work and employment have not been the route 'out of poverty' that the last two governments have insisted it is, with the lowest paid workers relying on government Working Tax Credits, Housing Benefit, and Council Tax Benefit to enable them to live even the most meagre of existences. It is the 'low pay, no pay' cycle which is causing the most harm, and misery, in poorer communities, rather than the government's false rhetoric of 'welfare dependency', 'broken families', and 'bad behaviour'.

Working-class 'bad' behaviour

Within the 'broken' Britain thesis there is clearly an argument that poor working-class people and neighbourhoods 'lack' what is needed to be of value. We might think of resources linked to the economy, such as employment, skills, and training. The discussion above shows that there are many families now lacking basic essentials to live a positive life. However, there is also an argument that 'lack' can be culturally pitched. Although throughout this book my main argument is that council estates should not only be seen as 'lacking', there are some areas in which they clearly are lacking. There is a definite lack of positive namings (images and narratives) and valuations of working-class practices and behaviours, particularly those situated within the unofficial community networks and the unofficial resources that are within poor communities and that often go undetected and under the radar of government scrutiny.

In later chapters it will be shown how the mothers on St Ann's estate who depend on state welfare benefits and live in council houses have an acute awareness of how they are often negatively viewed. Nevertheless, they are extremely active and work voluntarily, officially and unofficially, within their community, for the benefit of each other and for the community. Within the politics of social justice there needs to be an urgent address of how working-class neighbourhoods and communities are viewed, and that they should be represented in a more positive way and less as merely a utilitarian concern and/ or a drain on society, in addition to the structural and distributional issues of inequality. In order for us to understand how inequality seeps through the skin and into the fabric of a community, there needs to be better social and theoretical reflection. In particular, questions should be asked about the relationship between class inequalities and class differences, and also regarding class practices and the stigmatising of poor communities. The significance of those questions is to promote the idea that welfare policy needs to be more than just a means to an end. Policy needs to change its focus on changing (bad) culture and changing neighbourhoods from what is seen as unproductive and as made up of problem places and people. Instead, a different perspective is needed, and that is a process through which the goals of any government wishing to tackle inequality have a cultural merit and value beyond the economic.

Through the early work of Oscar Lewis in Mexico City in 1961 we can see how the practices of the poor become named as 'deficient' when trying to cope with the everyday stresses that being poor can bring. Lewis noted that some of the poorest people in Mexico City at the time had regular work, but many survived day to day through a miscellany of unskilled occupations, child labour, pawning personal goods, and borrowing from local moneylenders at exorbitant rates of interest. According to Lewis, they survived first and foremost because of their local social networks: family, neighbours and friends. Lewis described the social and psychological characteristics of what he calls the 'culture of poverty'. He also described other characteristics of this poor neighbourhood, which included being:

> ... distrustful of the basic institutions of the dominant classes, hatred of the police, and they are aware of middle class values ... but do not live by them. (Lewis, 1961, pp 26-7)

Lewis understood the actual living conditions of the poor, along with their everyday practices, as a 'culture of poverty'. He also noted that violence and abandonment of women and children were common and, as a result, mother-centred families and communities that had greater knowledge and ties to maternal relatives became the 'norm'. Lewis also argued that, within the 'culture of poverty', other traits developed:

> ... a strong present time orientation with relatively little ability to defer gratification and plan for the future, a sense of resignation and fatalism based upon the realities of their difficult life situation, a belief in male superiority which reaches its crystallization in machismo or the cult of masculinity, a corresponding martyr complex among women, and finally, a high tolerance for psychological pathology of all sorts. (Lewis, 1961, pp 27-9)

These traits then become the everyday practices of the community, and therefore the 'norm', passed on to each generation. It is almost the theory of 'if nothing changes then nothing changes', a common phrase which I have heard being used within Nottingham today.

The description that Oscar Lewis painted of this community in Mexico City is very harsh, but he also described a mutual solidarity among neighbours and moral obligations among family members. What Lewis described is a defensive value system created within this poor neighbourhood in order for that community to survive the extremes of social inequalities at that particular time in that particular place.

However, Lewis' theory of the 'culture of poverty' was misused by the UK Conservative government and the US neoliberal and right-wing social commentator Charles Murray in the 1980s in order to create their own theory of 'the cycle of deprivation' – the supposed perverse effects of welfare dependency – to implement neoliberal policies by rolling back welfare and state benefits and focusing on the family rather than the structural or societal causes of inequality.

Indeed, Oscar Lewis' work has been criticised as perpetuating the notion that the poor are responsible for their own poverty, especially through his theory of 'the culture of poverty'. The main criticism was that Lewis was only interested in 'third world' poverty, which did not translate over to Western democracies. Therefore, Lewis' theories, which were taken up by the US administration and used in social policy in the 1960s, particularly related to African American and immigrant communities, and were out of context in the US and did not factor in racism. Lewis was also criticised for the rise in the underclass theory, which had come out of the 70 indicators that he used to describe a community living with a 'culture of poverty'. According to the researchers Eames and Goode in 1977, the indicators had been used to collect statistical data to correlate poverty and deviance, rather than, as they argued, to 'make sense of the everyday actions of people in a context of extremely limited choices' (p 287).

There is no doubt that Lewis' work described a harsh and ugly view of being poor, violence, criminality, and abandoned families. However, what is often omitted when Lewis' work is discussed is his account of the strong, informal organisation of society, their resilience for finding solutions to their problems that the institutions often ignore. In a later work by Oscar Lewis in 1966, when he visited a slum district in Havana after the Cuban revolution, he noted that, even though conditions for the people were not dissimilar to the conditions he had witnessed before the revolution, and poverty still remained in the area, 'the culture of poverty' did not. Lewis concluded that hope had come into the people's lives, and hopelessness that he had witnessed earlier had dissipated even before a change in organisation had proved itself. Lewis argued in this later work that:

> By creating basic structural changes in society, by redistributing wealth, by organizing the poor and giving them a sense of belonging, of power of leadership, revolutions frequently succeed in abolishing some of the basic characteristics of the culture of poverty, even when they do not succeed in curing poverty itself.
> (Lewis, 1966, p 19)

I believe that there has been a genuine misreading by some, and a deliberate cherry-picking of Lewis' theory of the 'culture of poverty' by others. There has also been a major lack of understanding and a misvaluing of practices within poor communities in order to blame the poor for their poverty, and also to disguise the problems of the poor by problematising their spaces and behaviours. I think what Lewis was attempting with the 'culture of poverty' discourse was to examine the value systems that the poorest live within, thus attempting to make sense of and contextualising those everyday actions of people with limited choices because of the structure and the inequalities within their society, rather than purely examining the behaviour of the poor and blaming them for their situation, as he is often accused of doing. Being poor and working class means changing their practices and culture into something else more acceptable and less troublesome, without any consideration that working-class practices and culture have real value and worth in their own right. The negative valuing of working-class practices becomes reified, and negative meanings are attached to everything deemed to be working class; welfare policy therefore becomes purely prescriptive, one-dimensional and reduces poor neighbourhoods and their residents into one-dimensional subjects defined by 'lack', a position they can never really overcome.

The poorest groups and neighbourhoods within the UK, as has already been established, have been conceptualised, and known through many modalities, and the definitions constantly shift. Those definitions have led to specific and often negative understandings of poor working-class people, and it is through those negative definitions and damaging narratives that policies have been prescriptive regarding those who live in poor neighbourhoods. This book shows how the practices within poor neighbourhoods are immensely complicated, complex and rich, creating local processes and understandings and setting up local value systems which are often misunderstood, demeaned and ignored by those on the 'outside', thereby shaping those local value systems through their reactions to particular images and narratives. By examining the value systems that are alive in poor neighbourhoods, we can find out what is valued and important within. At the same time, we can distinguish what is missing within those neighbourhoods, and how the residents adjust their practices to compensate for what they do not have. While there is recognition that poor neighbourhoods and their residents have social, political and cultural needs that are often not being met, at the same time, there are local practices and processes that are working.

1

St Ann's, Nottingham: a working-class story

Introduction

In order to understand any neighbourhood, and the people who live in it, it is important to know the history of that neighbourhood, and the space that the people inhabit – not only their physical space, but also the space that they inherit, their social space. Within this chapter I introduce this neighbourhood of St Ann's, some of the characters that live within it, and I also outline the historical context that has shaped and continues to shape St Ann's and its residents.

This neighbourhood, like many poor neighbourhoods throughout the UK, has become stigmatised as valueless, broken, and 'wrong'. It has become typical in the UK over the last two generations to use the words 'council estate' to lazily explain a multitude of social problems, from housing and unemployment to low pay, criminality and failure. Council estates have therefore become sites of 'wrongness', with a focus on the people who live in them and their 'culture of lack'. If we are to believe our politicians, our media, and the multitudes of reality television programmes currently being shown on mainstream channels, such as BBC Two's 'We pay your benefits', Channel 4's 'Skint, benefits Britain 1949', and 'How to get a council house' (all of which were shown during July and August in 2013), people who live on council estates lack everything that is needed to become successful citizens in today's modern Britain. They lack aspiration, moral values, a work ethic, and are too located in the places where they live, leading to ignorance, stupidity, and lack of aspiration – they have become 'deficit' in the public imagination. The 'council estate' appears to have become the symbol of the Conservative Party's vision of what 'broken Britain' looks like, and residents of council estates have become, by their nature, the perpetrators of 'breaking Britain', and the cause of Britain 'staying broken'.

Against this backdrop of the 'broken' Britain rhetoric it is important to contextualise the actions and meanings of those who live on council estates, as without context, any social practice becomes awkward and difficult to read. Therefore, it is fundamental to place any neighbourhood, whether upmarket or deprived, within a sequence of historical change. Within any city it is only possible to understand any 'cross-sectional slice' of an urban neighbourhood by knowing the evolution of that social space, and the people within it.

It is important to know the neighbourhood and to orientate oneself within St Ann's council estate and also with its residents – it would be unfair and inaccurate to examine this 'slice' of a city in isolation, objectifying the neighbourhood and its residents, which is all too common in journalistic commentary about our most disadvantaged neighbourhoods.

By understanding the history of this estate and its residents, we can have a greater understanding of how this neighbourhood and its residents have, over time, managed the very difficult circumstances in which they have often found themselves. We can then begin to understand and open up debate about the consequences of these difficult circumstances, and the impact that living within a neighbourhood, which has been disadvantaged over an extensive period of time, has had on its current residents, as well as the consequences of long-term inequality on communities. To forget that urban space is a historical and political construction is to risk mistaking disadvantages, deprivations and stigmas as 'neighbourhood effects', which is nothing more than dividing society up according to economic and social differences, another way of socially reconstructing hierarchies within that society. Nevertheless, if we only treat this neighbourhood as an historical construction, it downplays the disadvantages that the neighbourhood has suffered, and does not truly show how those disadvantages manifest themselves within the neighbourhood through the residents' practices and their everyday lives.

This chapter shows how St Ann's, a neighbourhood housing the poor and the working class, has historically been regarded as little more than an overflow tank within an urban industrial city, which depended on industrial capitalism. Nevertheless, throughout history the neighbourhood and its residents have shown remarkable resilience, shape-shifting to the needs of a changing market, changing their practices in order to cope when capitalism has taken on different forms. Therefore, within the first section of this chapter I examine the history of the estate, its people, and how they have been positioned and known over time. In the second section I show the estate as it is today, through examining the local community, what services are in place, and how the estate is used and known.

Working-class Nottingham

Nottingham is the largest city situated within the East Midlands in the UK. It is the seventh wealthiest city in the UK, and was used during the New Labour years as one of the government's 'driver cities', an attempt to 'drive' some of the wealth and business opportunity northwards, out of the South East. Since the change in government during 2010, however, this has appeared less of a priority, with cities like Nottingham becoming visibly impoverished in a very short time, losing £100 million of central government funding since 2010, with another £25 million planned cuts for 2014/15 (Nottingham City Council, nd).

Nottingham and its surrounding county were built on heavy industry, a past created out of the wealth of coal mining, manufacturing, and engineering. Heavy industry and manufacturing work is embedded in its history, and also in the life of the working-class people employed within those industries. The history and significance of working-class Nottingham can be seen at almost every turn of a corner throughout the city. The architecture within the city has a very different look and feel to it than the finer, and more nuanced, architecture of some of its neighbours in the East Midlands such as Leicester and Derby. This is because Nottingham city centre was the hub of the manufacturing of lace, clothing and hosiery, and the large substantial factories and mills built predominantly in the 1840s are still within the city, albeit taking on a different role today. The city's Council House, which is situated in the centre, is a large, heavy, solid-looking building, with two unyielding stone lions which guard it on the newly rebuilt square. It is typical of the heavy, large, and looming symbolic structures of the power of local government more commonly found in northern cities such as Manchester or Leeds. The power and wealth within the traditional cities of the Industrial Revolution were generated by mine, mill and factory owners, who accrued enormous wealth in very short periods of time, and built gregarious structures to celebrate their success. These structures celebrating the success of early capitalism are noted throughout the City of Nottingham's history, and recognised through local walking tours and visitor information guides, but also, and more significantly, through their protection, by becoming listed buildings. However, the history of Nottingham and the successes that it enjoyed are also the history and the successes of the working class in Nottingham, albeit at the same time stark reminders of the massive wealth inequalities that have always existed in Nottingham.

The City of Nottingham began to thrive, as tens of thousands of workers poured into the city after the Enclosure Acts 1813-60, with Nottingham increasing its population from just 20,000 to 200,000 in the 10 years between 1821 and 1831 (Strange, 2007, p 114).

This left the city with a dilemma of what to do with their newly created proletariat workforce. Within the ward of St Mary, which is situated within the Lace Market (the site of many textile factories in Nottingham), there were as many as six families living within two-room dwellings, creating one of the most overpopulated and dangerous slums in the country at the time. After several serious outbreaks of cholera in the St Mary's ward, an area to the east of the city, known as the Clay Field, was used to bury the hundreds who died in the outbreak, but was also taken into the city boundary to house the proletariat workers and their families. This area was at the edge of the city and was very close to the Lace Market, and is now known as St Ann's, but originally it was called New Town because it was built and thought of as a new town within the city. New Town had been specifically built for the working poor, consisting of very basic workers' cottages, the largest number of public houses in the city, a bakers, a butchers, a marketplace and 'allotments'. The allotments started life as a green space situated between two of the three steep hills in the area. The workers were 'allotted' a slice of land where they could grow their own produce and continue their traditions of the rural life they had left behind. These were the first of their kind in the UK, and have now become a Grade II listed site by English Heritage. They are still worked on today by the local residents in St Ann's, and have become a treasured resource within the estate, one of the few historical tributes to working-class history in Nottingham.

New Town was a thriving area of the city for its new proletariat – the workers would be seen in their thousands leaving the area at dawn to go into the factories, and then returning again at dusk. Although they were not physically locked into their places of residence like the Jewish ghetto in Venice two centuries earlier, they knew that this was their place, a place of safety. Here there were no bosses, no 'coppers', and they were no longer under the intense scrutiny of the under-managers in the factories where they worked. The local constabulary in Nottingham never ventured into New Town – the residents 'policed' themselves through family affiliation and gang membership – and very few 'outsiders' were seen within New Town. It had a natural spring on its main thoroughfare going out from the city, called the St Ann's well. This was supposed to have healing properties and was well known to local women who drank from it, believing it especially aided fertility. Local women still believe today that 'there is something in the water', which perhaps explains why there have always been so many children in St Ann's.

By 1880, New Town had a new name, St Ann's, and the main thoroughfare where the well was situated became the St Ann's Well Road, as it stands today.

Neighbourhoods like St Ann's in Nottingham are often referred to inaccurately as 'ghettos'. Loic Wacquant, in his book, *Urban outcasts* (2008), discusses the history behind those places where the poor have been situated, and in particular, the concept of the 'ghetto', in order to understand disadvantaged neighbourhoods today. He argues that the 'ghetto' is a place where those are situated whose only value is their labour. However, the 'communal ghetto' is sharply bounded to a racial element: usually black workers bounded by a collective consciousness, and a near complete social division. It is acceptable to leave, but only to work, as their labour is needed and vital to the economy of the city. Wacquant argues that the 'ghetto' acts like a social condom, a way of allowing intercourse but without ever having to touch 'those who are unclean'; but it also acts as a screen to balance out some of the negative effects of 'inner-city' life (2008, p 2). Within the 'ghetto' the stigmatising effects of low pay and poor living conditions and class racism can be offset to some extent through the buffer of community and local culture. New Town in Nottingham, and then, when it later became St Ann's, was a place where the working poor lived, raised their families, engaged in their own cultural pursuits, and had little interaction except through work in other parts of the city. The labour of the residents within New Town/St Ann's was vital to the wealth and the economy of Nottingham.

Nevertheless, I would not go so far as to say that it was a ghetto within that period of time. Even though St Ann's, as it is known today, is often referred to as a 'ghetto', I believe that this is still an inaccurate definition, as there is high unemployment in the neighbourhood, and St Ann's has the highest number of Incapacity Benefit and Income Support claimants in the city (ONS, 2010). Indeed, Loic Wacquant might call St Ann's today a 'hyperghetto', a place where those whose labour has no value live, and the buffer against the negative effects of poverty and class racism have declined through the state's management of the poor.

'Whatever people say I am, that's what I'm not'

Poor neighbourhoods in Nottingham have always been notorious places, associated with danger, crime and sickness, such as cholera, and, more recently, obesity and mental health, but also resistance, from the Luddite uprisings, and the riots of 1832, in which the iconic and then hated Nottingham Castle was burnt down. However, one of the city's most famous and iconic anti-heroes came out of the pages of Alan Sillitoe's (1958) *Saturday night and Sunday morning*. During the 1950s many young authors began to note their experiences of working-class life in post-war Britain, and this novel contextualises the recent history of working-class Nottingham. Sillitoe depicts working-class life in one of the poor neighbourhoods in Nottingham in his semi-autobiographical, yet fictional, piece of work. Based on his own experiences, it is a relevant account, adding to this historical journey in understanding the poorest neighbourhoods in Nottingham and those who reside within them.

Sillitoe's anti-hero, Arthur Seaton, was one of the original 1950s working-class angry young men, working in the local factory, drinking and fighting in the local pubs, while enjoying the local countryside, a solace from the endless noise of the factory. Sillitoe captured working-class life in Nottingham in the 1950s with passion but also with a sense of fear – fear of what might happen to these incredibly complex but vulnerable characters. The people of Nottingham in Sillitoe's stories are vulnerable to their environment, but they are also angry: they are seething with anger at their unfair treatment by their bosses, the government, their cramped and inadequate homes, and mind-numbing and soul-destroying jobs. Many sociologists (Charlesworth, 2000; Walkerdine et al, 2001; Lawler, 2003, 2008; Skeggs, 2005; Reay, 2008), especially those few from working-class backgrounds, have complained that the seething anger that they have understood, witnessed and experienced as very much part of working-class life is often omitted or absent from academic research regarding working-class life. There can be no mistake that in Alan

Sillitoe's Nottingham there is seething anger and resentment, which often explodes into physical fights between both men and women, and their anger is very often turned on each other. Sillitoe does not objectify his characters, or glorify the ability of the working class to make virtue out of necessity, as other authors have done through condescending misunderstandings of just how difficult working-class life was, and still is. Arthur Seaton is neither a likable character, nor a working-class hero (whatever that term may mean). However, there is a complexity with how Arthur Seaton is presented and how this plays out in the relationship between his family, his employment, and the neighbourhood where he lives.

The lives and experiences of the history of women has traditionally been left out of depictions of working-class life, even though the women in St Ann's are central to its identity, and the community's sense of pride and resilience. The women in Sillitoe's depiction of Nottingham in the 1950s are fairly passive, but Sillitoe does briefly, although without any real awareness, show the subtle resistances in the way working-class women resist their positions. Arthur Seaton often complains, even 'hates the hard faced, grabbing women of Nottingham', women 'who you can't be nice to ... they won't let you'. He understands that the 'hard facedness' of the women in his life is the consequence of their hard lives. He hates the sadness and pain in his mother's and Aunt Ada's face and body as they move slowly through an unforgiving life, a life that has never forgiven them or let them forget that they are working-class women; their purpose, 'get a man, keep a man, have broods of kids, and make sure the dinner is alus on t' table'.

What Alan Sillitoe does is present a slice of the city's history through a very working-class method: 'storytelling'. However, this fictional piece of work is important to this contemporary narrative of council estate life: it traces a path of working-class life; it shows what effect living in poor conditions, working in physically demanding jobs, and having little expectation or opportunity has on communities, families and individuals. The narratives, and experiences, of those who live in St Ann's during the 2000s is also a working-class story, although many of today's residents talk of the difficulty of 'finding work'. bell hooks, the US black feminist writer, constantly argues that fictional stories within working-class traditions are ways of passing history down. She argues that 'storytelling' should not be ignored, especially when the authors are writing about their own locations – the 'stories', which have been written or told by minority and disadvantaged groups, may be the only record of how life is, or was, 'on the inside' (hooks, 1984).

Poverty: The forgotten Englishmen and '1968'

Storytelling has been an important method used by the men and women who have been part of this research to explain and tell their life histories. Many of those who have been involved in this research have lived on this estate for most or all of their lives. Some have family histories attached to this neighbourhood going back generations, and those whose families were not 'original' to St Ann's have similar stories of working-class families and life in other neighbourhoods around Nottingham, the Shire, and wider. The histories and stories of past working-class life were important to the residents in St Ann's. They told me of grandparents, and aunties and uncles, working at Raleigh Bicycle Company, or John Player & Sons cigarettes. They told of the social clubs they had been part of with their families, holidays in Skegness, the difficulties they had experienced as children, the poverty they remembered, and the hardships they and their families had endured. What had happened in their past was always important to their present story. When those stories of past working-class histories particularly relating to inequality and poverty are told through families, there is very rarely in-depth evidence of those inequalities, apart from memories, and sometimes photographs that families have held on to. St Ann's is an exception.

In 1968 two young researchers from the University of Nottingham, Ken Coates and Bill Silburn, boldly announced that 'poverty is back among us', even though Alan Sillitoe had written about poverty in Nottingham a decade earlier. They argued that during the 1950s there had been a myth that widespread material poverty had 'been finally and triumphantly overcome' (p 30). Rowntree and Lavers' report in 1951 concluded that poverty in most places had been reduced, and eradicated in the South East and Midlands due to full employment and plenty of overtime for men. However, there was a small group of persistent people at the time that constantly maintained that there was still a serious problem of material poverty, Peter Townsend being one of the most consistent and vocal. Coates and Silburn (2007) decided to conduct their own study in Nottingham to discover whether Townsend was right. The research focused on St Ann's. By this time it was an extremely poor and run-down area, the residents again living in slum conditions, situated three minutes from the city centre, and housing some 30,000 in the 10,000 two-up two-down back-to-backs which were prevalent all over the City of Nottingham. By 1968 the St Ann's area was approximately two miles in radius, with its boundary right on the city centre, as it has always been. Over a period of five years Coates and Silburn went around the estate with a questionnaire, interviewing residents, attempting to uncover the social and economic situation of the people of St Ann's. They also collected statistics and other information on housing in the area, such as the number of houses that had inside bathrooms and toilets, and other health-related statistics.

They found that only 9 per cent of the 10,000 houses had an inside bathroom or toilet, and over half of the properties had no hot water system installed, having to heat up water in pans on the stove for washing and bathing. They reported that many of the houses and yards (a yard being a block of 10 houses situated together and sharing an entrance, and often outside lavatories) had open Victorian drains, with waste running through at all times. There were rats in the houses, and disease and dysentery was a problem, especially for young children and the elderly. Infant mortality in St Ann's was running at three times the national average, and they discovered that this figure became worse when they studied the newly arriving West Indian families, who were often living in the worst conditions, suffering the most overcrowding. They also examined educational ability among children in St Ann's, and found that only half of the seven-year-olds in the neighbourhood could read. The schools were inadequate, having been built in the 1870s, and they were in the same run-down state as the housing. The teachers were 'well meaning, but had no sociological understanding of the neighbourhood' (p 132). In the research, published in 1970, Coates and Silburn did not directly address or analyse how the residents thought about themselves or their neighbourhood, rather focusing on the material consequences of poverty. Nevertheless, there is evidence within the research that the residents at the time had strong opinions of who they were, and how they were thought of.

Coates and Silburn asked their respondents how they thought of themselves in financial terms, and over 70 per cent 'did not see themselves as poor', with another 20 per cent describing themselves as 'hard-pressed'. Before Ken Coates sadly died in 2010, he and Bill Silburn talked about their research in St Ann's at public meetings, where they noted that this was always the most surprising part of the research, that the respondents who took part in the survey either did not want to tell the researchers from the University of Nottingham the full extent of their poverty or, as Coates and Silburn suspected, they simply had no way of comparing their own situation to another's. They thought this was the case because during the 1960s the people of St Ann's had very little interaction with anyone who lived in different circumstances to themselves.

The study was met with some anger through its publication in the local and national media, however, and a short documentary film was made and shown in 1970 about the neighbourhood and the research, featuring Ken Coates and Bill Silburn. After the film was shown and the research had been publicised in the *Nottingham Evening Post*, some of the residents complained that the research had 'shamed' the community by making them 'look poor'. One engineer, who was also a trade unionist at Raleigh Bicycle Company, complained that he was being made fun of by his work colleagues. He recounted his story in Ruth Johns' book, *St Ann's: Inner-city voices* (2002):

> I went to my lathe one day just after the poverty survey was in the post [newspaper], and there was half a boot strap on top, when I asked what it was some of my workmates said "It's for you poor fuckers as live in St Ann's." (p 223)

During 2007 the St Ann's documentary was shown again at the local arts cinema in Nottingham, and then within several of the community centres in St Ann's. Ken Coates and Bill Silburn attended the showings and were available for questions afterwards. I went along and they were well attended by local residents, past and present. All spoke of their hardships within St Ann's at the time, but they also spoke of the wonderful community spirit they remembered in the 1960s. Many of the residents thanked Coates and Silburn for the research and the documentary. It seems that much of the anger from 1970 had dissipated into a fond nostalgia of the past, and it is always easier on the soul to remember poverty than to be living in it.

By 1970, as *Poverty: The forgotten Englishmen* was published, the 10,000 houses in St Ann's had been earmarked for slum clearance, and many of the families were already being moved out to the larger, newly built sprawling suburban council estates on the outskirts of the city. Similar slum clearance programmes were occurring throughout the UK, from Glasgow down to the East End of London. Michael Young and Peter Willmott preserved their fears of the future for working-class communities in *Family and kinship in East London* (2007 [1957]), sometimes known appropriately as 'Fakinel'. Michael Collins (2004) and Lynsey Hanley (2007) have also recently mapped their own family histories of slum clearance to council estate in Birmingham and South London respectively.

What Coates and Silburn discovered in their original research in 1960s St Ann's was that this neighbourhood in Nottingham was part of a bigger picture of what was happening throughout the UK. The poorest people here were not 'work-shy' – in actual fact, there was very little unemployment in the neighbourhood – but poor housing and low wages were at the root of the neighbourhood's poverty and disadvantage. The poverty experienced in St Ann's in the 1960s was was hidden among the community and rarely seen by those on the outside of the neighbourhood. There was little understanding of how people on the estate lived. Indeed, Coates and Silburn reported a flagrant ignorance of the hardships that were being endured in St Ann's by other neighbourhoods in Nottingham, even those situated in close proximity. Their work in St Ann's was conducted during 1968, a revolutionary year where there were challenges to the existing social order in many parts of Europe and the world. The research took place at an intersection in history, not only through world events, but also local events. St Ann's was about to be demolished, and so was an inner-city working-class way of life. St Ann's was changing, and so was Britain.

Sunshine and rain: Jamaica comes to Nottingham

St Ann's began life as the place where the poorest – and, usually, those who were considered the most distasteful – of the city's population resided. It was also the place where those from outside of the UK came looking for jobs in Nottingham and would initially settle because of its low rents, and the residents' reputation for not asking too many questions. At the end of the 19th century there were many migrants from Scotland, Ireland and Wales coming to Nottingham looking for work in the textile and mining industries, and many settled in St Ann's because of its proximity to the Lace Market. After the First World War, Europeans came to St Ann's from Poland, Italy, and there were also Russian Jews. Many opened their own businesses in the neighbourhood and began the burgeoning and exciting trade in 'out of the ordinary goods' that St Ann's became known for and that Coates and Silburn wrote about in their research. However, most moved their families out of the neighbourhood as soon as they could afford better housing, and had learned how to mix within more affluent neighbourhoods, yet keeping their businesses in St Ann's. There was another large migration of Irish workers after the Second World War, again settling in St Ann's. However, they have stayed and have had an enormous influence within the neighbourhood, setting up Irish social clubs, and contributing to the two Roman Catholic churches on the estate. After the Second World War there was a new group of migrants in Nottingham, workers coming from the break-up of the British Empire from all over the West Indies. These migrant workers, like others, found the cheapest and most affordable places to settle, predominantly settling in St Ann's, Radford, and The Meadows areas of Nottingham throughout the 1950s until 1968, when the Immigration Act all but closed entry into the UK for West Indians. In St Ann's the first West Indian workers came in the early 1950s, increasing each year, and those settling in St Ann's were primarily Jamaican men, with Jamaican women following later. The 'small island people' (Barbados, Dominica, Trinidad, St Lucia) had settled in The

Meadows area of the city – this is said to be a factor in the ongoing rivalries between St Ann's and The Meadows.

The Jamaicans brought with them to St Ann's their culture and their vibrancy, their love of reggae and soca music and dance; their style, the men wearing stush and slick suits, the women wearing brightly coloured dresses more suitable for the Caribbean sun than the rain and smog of Alan Sillitoe's 1950s Nottingham; and exotic food such as yams and green bananas, and settled into the neighbourhood. Within a few years, they had set up food stores selling West Indian produce, their own churches, and the illegal and notorious shebeens (illegal gambling, drinking and dancing parties, later known as blues clubs). The black community in St Ann's also set up their own West Indian club, the WINA (West Indian National Association), which was eventually renamed ACNA (Afro-Caribbean National Artistic Centre), one of the first to be set up in the UK. In the early days of the 1950s it was a small office above the Co-op food store in St Ann's, the only organisation in Nottingham apart from the local Labour Party who were willing to give assistance to black people. WINA helped newly arriving West Indians to find a place to live and work, and gave them appropriate clothing as many had only their light-weight Caribbean clothing, inadequate for the UK at any time of year. Later they acquired premises, where they still hold wide-reaching community projects, from Saturday schools for black and mixed-race children, and lunch clubs for the elderly black community. Some turn into a night club in the evening, where local and Jamaican sound systems play, serving West Indian food and drink, and all of the community in St Ann's are welcome.

By the late 1950s and early 1960s the Jamaican community in St Ann's became stable as more Jamaican families moved in, rather than out, as previous migrant populations had done. There was another wave of Jamaican migrants in the early 1990s as existing and settled families became more affluent and began to send for their relatives – sometimes children they had left behind, or partners they intended to marry after visiting Jamaica. Consequently, today, many of the West Indian families are considered as 'old St Ann's' mainly because of the associations that the Jamaicans had with St Ann's before slum clearance, and in 2014, St Ann's is as much about being Jamaican as it is about the white working class. This was not always the case, however, as initially, the West Indian community and the white working class struggled to live side by side.

It was August 1958 and there was a reported disturbance in St Ann's at one of the local pubs, the St Ann's Inn on the Wells Road. By 1958 there was a substantial community of Jamaican men already living in St Ann's, and socialising in the local pubs. There had been some tensions in the neighbourhood about the numbers of single Jamaican men living in the area, with fierce competition for jobs and housing between the host community and the newly arriving West Indians, and also raw competition between the local 'Teddy Boys' and the Jamaicans for the attention of the local girls.

It was Saturday night, 23 August, when tensions exploded in the St Ann's Inn. Eyewitnesses at the time said that the trouble had started because there were two black men in the pub with white girlfriends, and as they left, the Teddy Boys insulted them. It was reported that the argument spilled out onto the street, and within an hour there were 1,000 people on the street, fighting, and damaging property.

The *Nottingham Evening Post* reported: 'The whole place was like a slaughterhouse, and many people were stabbed' (1958). There were reports at the time that the white Teddy Boys from Nottingham, who had been accused of instigating the disturbance, were carrying weapons – bike chains, knives, and machetes – but they were met by the young West Indian men with similar weapons. According to those who lived in St Ann's at the time, tensions had been rising for a while because some people in the white community felt outraged that black men were going out with white women. There were also frustrations within the West Indian community because they were struggling to find decent jobs as some Nottingham factories had refused to take black employees. Therefore, the tensions and frustrations of the poor living conditions in St Ann's, fear of falling down the social ladder even further by becoming unemployed, together with the racism experienced by the black community, and the anger over what were seen as the 'distasteful sexual practices' of some of the white women on the estate, exploded in 1958.

Ten years after those initial disturbances, Enoch Powell (1968) predicted 'rivers of blood' in the UK as he stated that the majority of migrants did not want to integrate and had their own agenda, 'with a view to the exercise of actual domination'. After this disturbance, the local West Indian community in Nottingham began to get involved in local politics, and backed the campaign for Labour councillors in St Ann's, which had traditionally been held by the Conservatives. This support has been a key factor for the continued success of elected Labour councillors representing St Ann's since 1970.

After the disturbance in St Ann's in Nottingham, many of the residents felt that the situation had gone too far, and there were enormous efforts by the local community to prevent such disturbances in the future. Local community leaders from the West Indian community and the white British community came together to discuss what could be done. The end result was ACNA, a social club in St Ann's, where the black community could socialise, and engage in education and training. Around the same time, the St Ann's Tenants and Residents Association (SATRA) was set up, initially to fight the demolition of St Ann's, even though they were unsuccessful. There has since never been any blood running through the River Trent in Nottingham and, since the disturbance in 1958, both the West Indian community and the white working class have successfully carved out a community in St Ann's.

Demolition and concrete

As 1970 approached, St Ann's Victorian back-to-backs came down, the cobbled streets were covered in tarmac, and there was a need for cheap mass housing throughout the UK's cities. Modernist interpretations vaguely linked to the works and writings of Le Corbusier's visions of homes and cities began to spring up all over the UK, from the Thamesmead estate and Trellick Tower in London, to Manzoni's concrete modernist dream of Birmingham. Local authorities on tight budgets have since been accused of plagiarising modernist theories on urban renewal which often failed to understand the essential humanism behind Le Corbusier's plans, and his would-be imitators led modernist architecture to being blamed for the problems of Western cities in the 1960s and 1970s. During this period the inner-city middle class moved out to the suburbs, leaving the poorest whites and minority ethnic groups within their new concrete estates. However, in St Ann's there had never been an obvious middle class, although all of the small businesses were run by independent and small business men and women often coming from the migrant population, who had made the area vibrant and colourful; but these businesses had also been demolished, and after that, they never returned.

St Ann's became one of those loose modernist projects of the 1970s, with its rows of prefabricated grey pebbledash housing. The estate houses 14,000 people today within a two-mile radius, and is still at the edge of the city centre. There are still some of the Victorian terraces mixed in with the grey concrete, sometimes privately owned, sometimes owned by housing associations or the local council; these are all that remains of the old St Ann's. The majority of the housing in the neighbourhood is council-owned; they are practical and simple blocks of housing constructed by Wimpey for low-income families. The original plan had been the 'Radburn Layout', which separates vehicles and pedestrians.

Even as the houses were going up there were deep concerns by the local people and SATRA about the lack of provision for different groups within the community, particularly the elderly. Local businesses from St Ann's were offered new units on the outskirts of Nottingham, in the newly developed industrial estates, many of which folded within a few years. Since 1970 millions of pounds have been spent on St Ann's through different government initiatives, such as the City Challenge programme and urban regeneration, in an attempt to put right the shortcomings of the original redevelopment of the 1960s and 1970s.

St Ann's in the millennium

The estate sits between two hills with a valley going through it. This main thoroughfare, the St Ann's Well Road, runs from one end of the estate into the city centre, effectively cutting the estate into two. The St Ann's Well Road was once a vibrant shopping area containing every shop that the neighbourhood needed and more, catering for the many different needs of its residents. Now it is a two-mile long soulless busy road leading out of the city for commuters. It is flanked by the low pebbledash houses on the left, and the backs of the multi-level flats and maisonettes on the right, all grey and all pebbledashed. Halfway up the road is the new doorless police station: all communication with the police takes place through the intercom at the side of the blacked-out windows. Robin Hood Chase (locally known as 'the Chase') sits to the side of the police station, once a Victorian pathway through a wooded copse – legend has it that Robin Hood and his merry men were often chased through this part of Nottingham, and now, ironically, it is the local precinct. Until 2011 it housed most of the community services and projects: Sure Start, the housing office, the doctors' surgery and health centre, a non-profit community laundrette and a post office. There was also a betting shop, a fish and chips shop, and the Co-op supermarket. In 2011 a new joint service centre opened and the doctors' surgery and health centre, library and housing office moved into this new shiny modern building. The community laundrette and Co-op supermarket closed in 2012, leaving the precinct with empty shop units and looking desolate. The launderette is now the St Ann's food bank, which has been very busy since it opened its doors at the end of 2012. It is next door to the Chase Fish Bar, which is owned and run by a local family who have had a chip shop in St Ann's since the 1960s. The Co-op is an empty unit. The community centre sits in the centre of the concrete precinct, and up until 2010 it was vibrant – you could buy West Indian food in the cafe, and many activities were held in the centre for the community, including the local Youth Inclusion Project. I have spent many hours during the last nine years in this centre, meeting, eating and talking with fellow residents. However, the centre has now been scaled down because of cuts in funding since 2010.

St Ann's library was also on the Chase and was extremely valued by the community: there was toddlers' storytime, ESOL (English for speakers of other languages) classes, and local councillors held weekly and well-attended surgeries; there was also the largest range of African Caribbean literature in the city. However, it is now part of the new joint service centre, and although the facilities are new and modern, there is something lacking. It is an institutional space; the connection to the community the old library had, where residents felt it belonged to them, has gone. The new library has security guards that patrol it, along with the waiting areas for health and housing services. The people who work in the library are behind a generic desk with other employees from the doctors' surgery and health centre and housing services, and they don't seem attached to the library as they once were – the residents have told me that 'they don't feel welcome here'.

Until 2010 the Chase (or the 'old precinct', as it is also known) was very busy in the day. And although there has been a rapid decline in services, a small market is still held here on Tuesdays, and the post office is still housed here, meaning that there are still mothers and children passing through, and pensioners collecting their money. Groups of local men stand outside the betting shop chatting, and it is often used as a meeting place for young people. This is, in fact, the only real community space on the estate, and has been well used in the past; unfortunately, it is now in severe decline, and the new multi-service centre does not 'belong' to the local community but to the people that work in it, and the security guards who patrol it.

The precinct closes down at night and becomes a very different space. It used to be the main site for drug dealing, usually heroin and crack cocaine, but even this trade has mostly moved to other parts of the estate. It is dimly lit, and has a real feeling of fear and insecurity; most residents avoid the area in the evenings. This space belongs to the street after dark, and if you are around and not recognised, you will be asked who you are and why you are there; if you are known, business will go on around you, socks will be pulled down and crack 'scored'. All this happens 20 yards away from the state-of-the-art police station and in front of the four centrally controlled CCTV cameras on each corner of the precinct.

The last pub in St Ann's closed during the summer of 2013, The Westminster – it has been partly demolished and there still remains a low wall where the car park used to be. Every day several local men and some women buy cans of extra strong lager and cheap cider from the shop across the road, and they sit drinking on the wall where the pub used to be, under a pub sign showing the Houses of Parliament.

If you move around the estate you realise that the old St Ann's that Coates and Silburn wrote about, with its narrow streets, haphazard layout, and confused, illogical planning, has been replaced with exactly the same, only in grey concrete: rows and rows of the same pre-built constructed grey concrete pebbledash houses, flats and two-storey maisonettes. These are suspended on footbridges on several levels, and reach each other through underpasses and subways, which are very often dark and covered in rubbish and debris. Between each row of houses are three-feet wide paths running down the back of the small square back yards – local people call them 'rat runs'. Many of these are poorly lit, and over the years have been one of the main sources of complaint from residents.

Phase 1 of the City Challenge programme in 1992 gated and walled off many of the 'rat runs' in an attempt to stop burglary, muggings, and sexual assaults on women in the area, but the gates and walls themselves have become a well-meaning source of aggravation for the neighbourhood. There is no direct access through much of St Ann's, and the gates act as a visual reminder that you are entering a neighbourhood that has a need for heavy gates, bars and locks.

Many of the addresses in St Ann's do not follow in any logical order, being built in blocks and rows facing each other; so one row of houses can belong to one street and the other block adjoining it to another, even though they are situated together, usually around a concrete-slabbed area. Many of the residents have complained about the difficulties in getting post and deliveries because of the complex nature of the addresses in the neighbourhood.

One of the reasons why the estate is difficult to access is because of the loose concepts of 'modernism' the planners were toying with at the time. The idea behind this was the 'Radburn Layout', a community without traffic. Hence, much of the estate is not easy to get to by car, and public transport does not go into the estate but rather through it. This has also left most properties on the estate without adequate parking or public transport for its residents. Vehicles are out of sight from their owners and susceptible to car theft and vandalism. There are also parts of St Ann's that are completely cut off from any amenities because they are positioned on the top of steep hills. Phase 10 of a five-year regeneration project has recently been completed, where one section of St Ann's has had its housing units literally turned around so the new fronts face the street; these were previously the backs of the houses. However, much of St Ann's still has a complicated and difficult layout, which has caused problems for deliveries of takeaway food, milk rounds and paper rounds; there have even been problems with taxis refusing to pick up and drop off in the neighbourhood, either through fear of crime, or the problems of leaving taxi drivers to find addresses.

St Ann's: a neighbourhood of disadvantage

St Ann's has some of the most serious disadvantages within the City of Nottingham, but is also one of the 10 per cent most deprived neighbourhoods in the UK. Life expectancy is only 68 for men and 76 for women, when the national average is 72 and 84 respectively (ONS, 2007).

Compared to other local authorities, Nottingham has the ninth highest percentage of 'under-20s' living in poverty. This rate is even higher for children under 16: Nottingham has the seventh highest percentage, with 32 per cent classified as 'living in poverty' – a total of 18,840 children in 2010 (Nottingham City Council, 2012). In both age groups, only London authorities and Manchester have higher rates of child poverty. Between 2009 and 2010, despite a small reduction in child poverty rates, Nottingham's position relative to other authorities worsened. The experiences of parents are shaped by the local employment market, financial exclusion, economic recession, national changes to welfare benefits, adult literacy levels, the availability of good quality affordable childcare, by fuel poverty, housing and environmental issues, parental physical and mental health, and more.

St Ann's also has the highest number of people not employed within the city. This includes 1,278 people claiming Jobseeker's Allowance, with a total of only 42 per cent of St Ann's residents in any kind of employment, 15 per cent of those unemployed being over the age of 50, 10 per cent never having worked, and 40 per cent being the long-term unemployed. Recent figures (Nottingham City Council, 2012) have also noted that St Ann's has the highest number of Incapacity Benefit claimants, with 19 per cent of St Ann's' population claiming. A report, drafted by Nottingham City

Council as the *Local government learning plan* (2008), also examined the ethnic composition of unemployment particularly for young people aged 16-24, and showed that there are large variations between the different ethnic groups, with the mixed-race and Afro-Caribbean population faring badly.

Educational achievement

Educational achievement has long been considered an indicator showing the affluence of a neighbourhood, but also how a neighbourhood fares more generally. The *Local government learning plan*, prepared by CLES for Nottingham City Council, a local government consulting agency, in order to 'provide strategic responses' to St Ann's regarding employment and education, used Census data, and locally collected data in 2007, in addition to the Learning and Skills Development Agency (LSDA) report *Widening participation* in 2007. They discovered within this report that one of the key problems in St Ann's was a 'culture of low aspiration and low confidence' (LDSA,2007).

Local schools

The estate is served by four primary schools, which were built after the slum clearance programme, and the secondary school was opened in 1966; in 2009 it became part of the Nottingham Academy. The infant and primary schools (which took academy status in 2012) have been ranked by Ofsted (2012) as 'outstanding' in some areas of their teaching practice and methods, especially in key subjects. The Ofsted report also acknowledged the work being done at primary level around children's wellbeing, and the high commitment to inter-cultural teaching – the schools in St Ann's were reported to be 'outstanding' in these areas. However, Ofsted also reported and recognised the high levels of deprivation and the social disadvantages that the children on the estate were experiencing. They reported that two thirds of all pupils in primary schools were eligible for free school meals. This is more than twice the national average, and is a key indicator for showing poverty levels within families. Almost three quarters of the pupils were from minority ethnic groups, either African, Afro-Caribbean, a small number of Asian, and Chinese, and the largest ethnic group were mixed race. Over a quarter of the pupils coming from minority ethnic groups did not speak English as their home language. The report noted that almost two thirds of the pupils had special educational needs or disabilities; this is much higher than the national average. This level of special need varied from 50 per cent of pupils to 90 per cent in different year groups, which the report noted was 'alarmingly high' (Ofsted, 2012).

Ofsted also reported that the children entering nursery schools in St Ann's had skills and abilities that were well below average, in particular, in speech and communication, and in their social and emotional development. Nevertheless, when the pupils in St Ann's were tested in Year 7 by national SATS (Standard Assessment Tests), the results showed that 80 per cent of the children in primary school tested at Level 4 or above in key subjects, in comparison to children schooled within West Bridgford, the wealthiest neighbourhood in Nottingham, and the constituency of the Conservative Member of Parliament and grandee Kenneth Clarke, where 98 per cent of the children scored Level 4 or above. This shows that the children in St Ann's, despite their disadvantages, when entering nursery school have begun to make headway within their educational abilities

However, by the age of 12, when tested at senior school, only 54 per cent of children from St Ann's scored Level 4 or above compared to 89 per cent of pupils attending a similar size comprehensive school in West Bridgford. The picture continues to deteriorate by the age of 16, when only 7 per cent of pupils at the local comprehensive school in St Ann's achieved five or more 'good' GCSEs. Almost all students at the West Bridgford school achieved at least five higher grade GCSEs in 2011, and 90 per cent did so including English and mathematics. While the secondary school in West Bridgford has a majority of white British students, the Ofsted report in 2011 discovered that there were at least 50 languages identified at the Nottingham Academy in St Ann's. Ofsted noted that there had only been 29 different languages identified four years previously, and over that period there had been a marked increase in immigration into the neighbourhood, particularly from those coming from Eastern Europe, Somalia and the Middle East.

The Ofsted report clearly shows that children enter nursery schools in St Ann's already disadvantaged through poverty, lack of communication, and social skills. However, by the age of seven there are real improvements, and many of the children in this neighbourhood make up considerable ground in their educational attainment, despite being surrounded by the social disadvantages within their neighbourhood. SATS results then show that these improvements diminish over the years, and the disparity between children by the age of 16 living in wealthier neighbourhoods in Nottingham, such as West Bridgford, and those living in St Ann's is enormous (Ofsted, 2012).

Local services

There are two youth clubs on the estate. One is the Sycamore Centre run by a community voluntary organisation; they have a volunteers shop open in the daytime, training, and educational adult advisers, and also small business advisers. The other is a local authority-run youth club, which has a music studio. The Youth Inclusion Project was run from Robin Hood Chase community centre until it was severely scaled back because it lost its funding in 2010. Similarly, the Flower Girls course was also held there, teaching flower arranging, and there was a community non-profit-making florist on the Wells Road where the Flower Girls could volunteer and gain work experience; unfortunately, these services have also now gone from the community.

Service providers tend to bid to provide services in the local neighbourhood and then come into the neighbourhood, setting up various projects. The emphasis is on the services being delivered within the estate: education for young people and adults, training, and also volunteering. The focus during the New Labour years, 1997–2010, was to bring services to the community rather than encouraging the people of St Ann's to seek support outside of the estate. There has always been a significant focus around 'volunteering', and many projects have been set up within the neighbourhood encouraging residents to volunteer, usually within the neighbourhood itself.

Opportunities to volunteer are focused on youth and community work, befriending, working in the cafe in the community centre, working on the allotments, and being part of the Flower Girls. The emphasis is around work experience, which, according to the agencies involved, could eventually lead to paid work.

The emphasis on paid work within the neighbourhood is hardly surprising, as the local authority has identified St Ann's as 'a high pocket of unemployment', even though unemployment rates have risen within the city more broadly in recent years.

St Ann's, Stannzville, SV

The very words, 'St Ann's', have the ability to evoke many thoughts and feelings by the people of Nottingham, from those who call St Ann's home, to those who believe it is hell. According to records as far back as 1880, the St Ann's neighbourhood has always had a reputation for crime and 'villainy'. There were also reports of gang membership and family association linked to specific forms of violent crime at the end of the 19th century. Prostitution has been associated with the neighbourhood for many generations, as Nottingham's red light district is on the edge of St Ann's, and it was also the neighbourhood in which most of the city's 'poor' and migrant populations have settled, adding further stigma through the fear and development of the 'other'.

Therefore, the neighbourhood's reputation has always preceded it, and the words 'St Ann's' today conjure up strong thoughts and feelings among Nottingham residents in a way that no other neighbourhood has the power to do. St Ann's has recently been linked again, usually through the moral panic of media representation, as an area ridden with crime, drugs, gangs and guns, following the high profile murders of several teenagers on the estate: Brendan Lawrence aged 16 in February 2002, and the widely publicised murder of 14-year-old Danielle Beccan in October 2004. Both were victims of drive-by shootings. Like other inner-city neighbourhoods in the UK, there have been many incidents of stabbings and shootings linked to gang involvement between rival gang members from St Ann's, known as Stannz, Stannzville or SV, and other neighbourhoods in the city. It is not unusual as you walk around St Ann's to see unofficial memorials set up around the estate in the form of flowers, scarves, teddy bears, and graffiti for the many dead children and young people who have lived and died on the estate. This has led to an attack by the media on the City of Nottingham and in particular the St Ann's area through headlines in the tabloid newspapers such as 'Shottingham' and 'Assassination City' (*The Sun*, 22 October 2004). The BBC's Newsnight programme in 2003, even before the Danielle Beccan murder, labelled St Ann's a 'sink estate' and one of the 'most violent estates in the UK' after showing footage from a home security CCTV camera sent to them by a resident of a gun battle outside his home (BBC Newsnight, 2003).

The number of shootings peaked in 2004, with 42 incidents reported to the police, and since then there has been fewer high profile incidents in the city. The media has since moved on, focusing its attention instead on the constant reporting of gang-related violence and youth crime in other areas of the UK. Even though there are still shootings and stabbings in Nottingham related to 'estatism', those incidents mainly go unreported. However, during the 2011 summer disturbances that took place in many English cities, in Nottingham, many of those arrested for 'rioting' lived in the St Ann's area.

At the beginning of this chapter I set out to show the incredible history within this stigmatised urban space in Nottingham. I wanted to explain how over time the neighbourhood and its people have suffered from the triangular relationship of the state, social positioning, and the flux of an urban capitalist environment, focused on the needs of capital rather than people. We can see how Nottingham as a small insignificant city in early capitalism benefited enormously from the labour, culture and achievements of the working-class people who lived within its boundary. By mapping out the history and culture of those whose toil and hardship allowed the city to grow and become prosperous, we can acknowledge the incredible strength, vitality and the will to survive that the poorest residents of this city have within their history.

There are many ways of mapping a city's history and achievements: Nottingham is full of 'walking tours' around the Castle and the Lace Market, where we can wonder at 19th-century industrialism and

21st-century 'city life'. However, very rarely is a city's history mapped through the everyday lives of those who have gone unacknowledged for generations, and who are still barely acknowledged today, and even then only through reports showing their 'lack of' everything, from education, employment, culture, and morality. What this chapter has attempted to do is to orientate the reader, allowing the reader to understand this neighbourhood as it stands today, but also the interwoven experiences of the many different lives that have passed through it, creating a neighbourhood that is disadvantaged in many respects, but that also has advantages of a long history of migration, the sharing of cultures, and some of the most interesting and kind-spirited people you could ever meet. As you sit waiting to a see a doctor in the local health centre for a minimum of two hours every appointment because of the incredible lack of resources, where there are patients from all over the globe struggling with the NHS system, every day an old Jamaican man comes in and sings a round of old Jamaican Ska songs to entertain the patients as they wait. He gets a round of applause, and leaves, always to return the next day.

2

'Being St Ann's'

Getting by, by making ends meet

Growing up in a working-class family and on a council estate, I have heard and been part of many conversations among women regarding childcare, child development, running a home, handling relationships, budgeting, and in general, simply 'making ends meet'. I know these conversations are not limited to working-class women who live on council estates; however, included in these conversations are other aspects of family life, which are particular to where you live, and where in society you are positioned. Passed-down knowledge has always been important among women, particularly when that knowledge is about 'making ends meet', or 'getting by'.

'Getting by' comes in different forms, from where you can buy the cheapest chicken, to how you might handle the various government agencies you have to deal with, often on a daily basis. As a woman living on a council estate it is important to know 'what to say' and how to answer a question – answering a question 'wrongly' can have steep penalties.

There is one topic of conversation I have heard throughout my life, first hearing it as a child listening to my mother and aunties. I was about seven years old and I used to listen to them talking on a Saturday afternoon in our living room. They didn't notice me listening in as long as I sat beyond the boundary of eight women chain smoking John Player Specials; I could, as we used to say, 'tab hang' into their conversations. After my grandparents' death, my mother had been forced to go to what was then National Assistance; she had to give up her job making tights in a factory to look after her younger sister, brother and me. The conversation, as I remember, was that they had refused her claim for assistance, on the basis that she was a single mother, and young – they suggested that she, 'as a young girl could sell her clothes, and records'. Since that time I have heard this conversation about 'asking for help' and how to deal with the benefits agency many times over several different generations of women. It is part of 'the conversation', in how you learn to 'get by'. Being able to negotiate your way around the welfare system and knowing how to 'answer questions' is part of your education; I think my mother found out that answering questions 'wrongly' had severe consequences.

Lesson one of the 'knowledge' is that the people who work in welfare benefits offices are nosey and want to get their noses stuck into your business; this is a mortal sin in working-class neighbourhoods. Although everyone knows everyone else's business, you do not overtly seek it out, or directly ask questions. There are ways of finding out what you need to know within any estate, which allows sensitivity to another's private business, and private troubles. It is therefore 'common knowledge' that those who work in 'official institutions' linked to welfare benefits are trying to catch you out – they are sneaky, and they appear to have a particular understanding of women who live on council estates. As one young mother told me, "they start working you out on sight." Consequently, women pass on 'the knowledge', which is valuable for 'how to answer questions'. This is particularly striking within the line of questioning about who you live with, and your relationship with a child's father. When claiming any welfare benefits there are mandatory questions about personal relationships, a child's father, and the father's responsibility to financially support the child. Most women who have been part of this research have complex and sometimes difficult relationships with their children's father; I discuss the reasons behind some of those complexities in more detail in the next chapter. But here, I want to explain the process of negative representations, of how you are represented and how you have to represent yourself in order to simply 'get by'.

In the 1980s and 1990s, as a single mother claiming any type of benefits, you were always called in to the benefits agency for 'an interview' where you would be asked detailed and very personal questions about your child's father; this has been replaced more recently with telephone interviews. Starting with his name, where he lived, where he worked, and then what he looked like, a description was always needed. If you failed to give a name and address, your benefits would be stopped. This seems simple – why wouldn't a woman want to give the name and address of her child's father? Why shouldn't he be responsible for his child? When you are trying to 'get by', however, life is far more complicated than simply what might appear to the rest of the population as morally right or wrong. There is a line in the song 'It's a fine life' sung by Nancy in the musical version of Charles Dickens' *Oliver Twist*, 'Oliver!'; it has always struck me as explaining a lot in a few words:

> Who cares if straightlaces sneer at us in the street, fine airs and
> fine graces, they don't have to sin to eat. (Bart, 1962)

This is the message that women who live on council estates often tell. The first casualty of being a working-class woman in order to 'get by' is your respectability. If you receive welfare benefits, you will not receive money collected from your child's father by the Child Support Agency. This money goes straight to the benefits agency and into the central coffers of the Exchequer; therefore there is no direct benefit for the mother or the child. Women are therefore reluctant to give the names of their children's fathers to official institutions – it is intrusive, and there are many reasons why they may not want to: some women have very good relationships with the children's fathers and are still in close relationships with them; the mother and father can still be in a relationship although they may not live together on a full-time basis; and some women have private agreements with their children's fathers that benefit the mother and children directly – I know of a father who buys his children most of their clothes and shoes. If the Child Support Agency was involved, however, this money would go directly to the agency and not to the children.

There are other women who have very bad relationships with their children's fathers, and to get the Child Support Agency involved would be very stressful in some cases, and dangerous in others. Consequently, for most women on benefits, declaring the name of their child's father to the Child Support Agency is not beneficial; it is difficult, and it can be stressful. Therefore the women on the estate pass around the information of 'what to say'. There are many women who have had to say at benefit agency interviews that they do not know who their child's father is – he was a one-night stand, and they can't remember his name. This is where the benefits agency asks for a description, and women have told me that they fabricate one. This is humiliating and difficult for every woman I know who has had to do this, but as they told me, it is the only way 'to get them off your back'.

I have been in the company of groups of women who have recounted this situation in many ways. Yvette, a woman in her thirties who has three children, told a group of us while we were in the community centre that when asked to describe her baby's father, she described him as a 'hunchback with one eye'; as we all laughed at this, she said the woman interviewing her had to write it down. The thought of the woman in the benefits agency having to write down 'hunchback with one eye' caused fits of uncontrollable laughter. Yvette felt she had won a small battle that day by using humour, and 'taking the piss'. Nevertheless, this does not diminish the fact that women who claim welfare support and live in social housing pay the price for this difficult existence through humiliation and being disrespected.

This chapter focuses on the stigma that is associated with St Ann's, how it is viewed and known throughout wider Nottingham, and also how those who live in St Ann's have been stigmatised by association. The women describe this as 'being looked down on' while the men accept the reality of living in the 'endz' and how they 'work around it'. However, it is the women who live in St Ann's who have the most acute awareness of how they are known and represented in Nottingham and beyond; they explain how 'others' think they are 'rough and ready'. This term was used by many of the women in explaining how they thought 'others' saw them, 'rough' meaning violent, aggressive, and dirty, while 'ready' means sexually available. They explained this to me as, "You know, the women who tell their kids to fuck off in the social. Well that's what they think we are."

The women talked about their lives, and described how they thought they were excluded, looked down on, and demeaned. They discussed these dimensions of exclusion in the way they felt disrespected, and also how they thought the neighbourhood was disrespected. This often gave rise to feelings of fear, hostility and anger towards those they believed 'looked down on them', but also towards themselves through their powerlessness in trying to change the situations that hurt them.

The men described their relationship to the estate very differently, in particular, how they thought 'others' saw them. While the women were aware of their high visibility – in that they live in the public sphere of government agencies, schools, healthcare, and they move around the estate with their children – the men rarely thought about their public profile outside the estate. In effect, the men tried to be invisible on the outside. It took many questions to initiate any discussion with the men about those who did not live on the estate, or those they had no real relationship with. The levels of fear and exclusion that are experienced in this community also affected issues of mobility, the difficulties that sections of the neighbourhood had in moving in and out of the estate, but also the difficulties that arose from having real emotional attachment to a place, therefore not only belonging to St Ann's, but 'being St Ann's'.

Starting out

I started this research in 2005, initially focusing on women on the estate, and in particular, white mothers with mixed-race children. From the first time I came across Ken Coates and Bill Silburn's book, *Poverty: The forgotten Englishmen*, I wanted to tell my story of council estate life from the position of both a working-class woman and a resident of the estate. I focused on white mothers with mixed-race children living on the estate. I had noticed over the many years I had lived in the neighbourhood that there were a significant amount of women like me, who were white and had mixed-race children. And if you want to know anything about a neighbourhood, ask the women, especially the mothers, as they spend much of their time in and around the estate, taking children to school; they are also heavily invested in the neighbourhood, usually through family and kinship networks – what matters to the community matters to the women who raise their children in it.

I met the women in many community spaces – it wasn't difficult to meet them, and it wasn't difficult to find them. However, it was difficult to gain their trust and acceptance. Even though I had lived on the estate for over 20 years, the women did not welcome me into their lives with open arms. They were initially sceptical – what did I want to know about them? Why did I want to talk to them? What would happen? And was there any point? More importantly, most people in St Ann's were acutely aware that asking questions in the neighbourhood usually led to the neighbourhood being represented negatively, or 'outsiders' using local knowledge for their own benefit.

So I used my own local knowledge of the networks already in place to meet and talk to residents. I approached established groups and projects. The Chase community centre was a good place to meet – it was central, and on the local precinct where the Co-op, doctors surgery, library and housing office were situated. The women spoke to me in groups. I met them for coffee in the community centre, and they began to 'vet me'. I was finding out about them, but they were also finding out about me – they probably knew much more about me than I them. Within a few weeks we knew how we were connected to the estate, and how we might have connections to each other.

Being connected, and finding connections, these are important when you live on a council estate, and this was very familiar to me. It is a practice that I have been part of all of my life, so finding connections and networks in an ethnographic research context was not difficult. Part of the network practice is discovering which school you went to, who your parents were, grandparents, where you had lived, which pubs you had drunk in. The outcome of this process, and usually the unspoken aim, is to find out that somewhere along the way you have connections and possibly even family and kinship ties. I had not grown up on this estate but had come to St Ann's as a young mother with my baby son. My child's father and his extended family were well known and established on the estate, however, so we found our connections through our children. My son had gone to school with some of their children, I had friends who were friends with their friends, and the extended connections and networks were formed.

Communities are complex, and without understanding the context of people's practices, what they do can be misinterpreted, and misunderstood. This is where, again, I have to stress the importance of narrative, and where ethnography as a research methodology is valuable when studying communities. There are many ethnographic studies that have been re-visited generation after generation, and there are always important and rich findings that tell us about our society through the lens of the local community. *Family and kinship in East London*, by Young and Willmott (2007 [1957]), is a brilliant example of how important local community studies are to understanding the inequalities and problems for some in our society. In-depth study into a local community can also capture the strength and resilience that are usually buried very deeply within a neighbourhood, and are often missed or discarded, especially within political, policy and media rhetoric about poor neighbourhoods.

Small stories

When you spend as much time on this particular council estate as the women who live on it do, it can be easy to miss or diminish some of the real and everyday problems within the estate caused by the original planning and building during the 1970s. This is because you learn to cut through the estate, weaving in and out of the alleys, across slabbed and concrete squares in order to reach your destination as quickly as possible, rarely taking the time to look at what is around you. You often accept the things that are not possible within this context because it has always been so, or has been so for as long as you remember. In particular, I am thinking about getting a taxi to pick you up from your own address, or to take you home to St Ann's after a night out, or having a pizza delivery to your home, or even being able to see your car from where you live. These are the types of things that most people take for granted about the place or community in which they live.

The opposite can be said to be true here – what happens here in St Ann's is that you take for granted the things that you are not able to do, and there is a grudging acceptance that after a certain time in the evening, you cannot get a taxi to pick you up, or have a pizza delivery. This grudging acceptance of all the things that you cannot do because of the physical restrictions on you by the way the estate has been planned and built was generally acknowledged throughout the community and has always been a topic of conversation within the neighbourhood. The physical restriction and the obvious disadvantages that come from living on poor council estates seems to be an appropriate place to start in examining and opening up debate about the particular disadvantages the women I spoke to experience within this community, as it was one of their main concerns about where they lived.

If we are to discuss how and why some groups are disadvantaged in our society, simple things such as having a pizza delivery appear to be unimportant and insignificant. However, it is this type of small issue that has a big impact on a community, especially when it seems that everyone else can have this service except for you. All of the women I spoke to complained about not being able to have the things that 'others' have:

> "Yeah it's hard to get deliveries down this part because they have to get out and then they can't find your house, they tried to charge me once 'cos they couldn't find the house ... since the milkman got battered it's hard to get anything to come down here."

> "I know they will deliver to the students on the bottom of Wells Road, I've seen 'em."

The women who live in St Ann's know that the neighbourhood has become restricted from receiving various services because of the notoriety of the community, and also because of the high levels of crime. The name 'St Ann's' and what that means locally also puts restrictions on this community; nevertheless, they are acutely aware that others who share part of their living space (such as students) are seen and treated differently.

During 2007 I was out canvassing for the local council elections with a group of women I had met – they were all residents of St Ann's and were helping their friend campaign as a local councillor. We were targeting specific addresses in order to deliver leaflets and to talk to residents. This is not easy in St Ann's. In fact, sometimes it was near impossible – the houses are built in such a way that there are blocks of four to six houses in a row, and there are usually four rows of houses facing each other rather than facing the road, with a 3ft wide alley (the 'rat runs') at the back of each row, where another set of houses backs on. The estate appears to be a large two-mile radius concrete maze. Many of the rows of houses do not have the same address – one row can belong to one street address, another row to another. Almost everything on the estate is grey concrete, and there is little access for cars once you get within the estate.

As we walked and talked our way around the estate, we found that there were real difficulties in just moving physically through the estate, especially if you had a pushchair, because of the many barriers, gates, walls, and blocks of concrete in the pavement attempting to stop mini mopeds and scooters. Many of the residents we spoke to complained about the difficulties in getting post and deliveries because of the complex nature of the addresses in the neighbourhood. One of the women suggested that the architects 'must have been on crack'; we all agreed while laughing at the idea of an architect sat in his office smoking crack and designing council estates for us to live on – it seemed as rational a response as any other to the irrationality of the neighbourhood layout.

I have kept a research diary over the last nine years, and still keep it today, partly out of habit, but also because I know there is much more to say in the future about council estates, which I intend to say. Sometimes re-reading my diaries and going through those conversations can be uneasy. For example, I wrote in my research diary at the time:

> As we laughed and talked about crack-addicted architects on the pipe, I was thinking is this an average and normal conversation, do other people laugh about the crack pipe? – most of us knew someone who was addicted to or had been addicted to crack and we were laughing our heads off. (diary entry dated 29 April 2007)

There were many conversations about drugs, prison, prostitution and varying levels of crime that we offhandedly spoke about, laughed at, and gossiped about. It was only when I was alone with my own thoughts and the research diary that I reflected on those conversations, often in comparison to the very different conversations that I overheard, and sometimes joined in with, at the university. It was at those moments that I felt extreme despair at how we, in St Ann's, had normalised our own and others' social problems, took the blame for them, and blamed others, while laughing at some of the ridiculous situations we were often faced with. I have many examples of serious situations that I have recounted to those who do not live on the estate, or who have not lived on council estates, who wince at these stories, which I sometimes think are funny. It is these situations that I struggle and have struggled with, with my own insider/outsider position. I have asked many times, should I tell these stories, and also, should I make light of them? However, 'giving good banter', and being able to tell a good story, is both an art form on council estates, and also necessary as part of 'belonging' to the estate.

When the estate was built in the 1970s the issues that the residents faced because of the difficult layout were thought to be teething problems, and they would become used to the 'modern design' within time. Many of the women I spoke to who had lived in St Ann's as it was built talked of their mothers' pride about their 'posh homes' and the sense of worth they had in this new and modern community, with new schools, new shops, a new library, and a new Co-op supermarket. They remember this time as an exciting and modern community, moving into the 1970s and out of the poverty and squalor of the two-up two-down terraces. However, over time, the estate began to lose its grey concrete shiny newness, and with the1980s came dark nights, and dark times, rising crime, and the damp and brittle walls returned to the new houses, as they had in the old terraces. The estate and its residents were not equipped for the deep 1980s recession that ripped through the East Midlands, with the loss of manufacturing industries and coal mining. The young and first generation of black Britons that Paul Gilroy writes about in *There ain't no black in the Union Jack* (2000), were equally unprepared for the deep and institutionalised racism that was inherent within the fabric of British social structures, and became all the more vicious within the 1980s economic recession. The neighbourhood had high unemployment, particularly among the young people on the estate, and became susceptible to crime; the narrow and poorly lit alleyways and its complicated street plans only added to the problems. In the early 1990s the local council countered this by blocking off the walkways, and setting in heavy gates and high walls so it would be more difficult for those who wanted to burgle homes to have access to the backs of the houses; they also cut off many of the alleys with high metal railings because of the increase in street robberies and sexual attacks on women.

Extremely high metal gates started to appear around the local schools and other official buildings, as did the many eyes of the CCTV cameras during the early 2000s. My own son was a casualty and has since become an urban legend at the 'hands' of one of those high metal fences. During his last year at secondary school he attempted to climb over the fence at lunchtime, trying to 'escape'; he was wearing a ring on his middle finger which caught the metal fence, and as he jumped from the 5ft fence, his finger and the ring did not go with him. His finger (or its remains) was never found, and the myth began that an urban fox had come on to the school premises and had eaten it. Consequently, at the start of each new school year, my son's unfortunate story is used as a warning to children, not to jump over the fences, and not to wear jewellery at school.

There have been other consequences of those metal gates, locks and fences, which are less obvious and far more complex than the hazard they may cause unruly council estate children trying to 'escape'. During a visit to one of the local primary schools at lunchtime, I was waiting with one of the women while she picked up her children. We sat in the playground with her five-year-old who had just started school, and her three-year-old who was at nursery. We took photographs together of what we could see in and around the playground. Sitting on the floor so I could be at the same height as the children, we looked at the City of Nottingham in the distance through the metal fence – we could see the children's homes, the park, and the police station. When looking at the images afterwards that the children had taken, I was staggered by them, and consequently the lens through which these very young children saw their neighbourhood and their city – through the criss-cross of a metal fence, through bars, locks, and heavy gates. If you did not know what you were looking at you could be forgiven for thinking that the images had been taken from the exercise yard of a prison.

The older children on the estate learned how to 'use' their environment; they told me about the games they had made up 'playing with the CCTV cameras', getting the camera to follow them by putting their hoods up on their tops and coats, and running, all at the same time. If there were enough of them and they were well coordinated, they could sometimes get the police helicopter to follow them using the same method.

The residents I met, and indeed my own experience of the estate as a resident, was that although the estate was difficult to live on and to move around in, it seemed that the blocks of concrete, metal railings, gates and locks were necessary evils, otherwise the other option was to knock the whole place down, which was always a constant fear for those living in St Ann's. This fear often came up in conversations about the estate, and in particular the future of the city – the estate sits right next to the thriving city centre of Nottingham, and residents were in constant fear that one day the city might need their estate to continue and extend the growth of the commercial centre. Each time there is an incident on the estate because of planning, or because of the changes that have been made to the estate in order to make it 'safer', the residents fear that the council might give up on them, and decide to knock the whole thing down, which would be devastating.

I met two sisters, Della and Julie; they had lived on the estate from being children, and now in their thirties, they both rented their homes from the council. Della had five children and Julie had two, and both identified themselves as 'single mums'. They told me of an incident in which the milkman had been beaten up quite badly and robbed early one morning amid the maze of St Ann's:

> "... and 'cos of that now we can't get delivery people down here 'cos we've had pizza people battered down here as well."

Julie and Della were really angry about the situation, and also 'felt sorry' for the milkman, as well as the older people on the estate. They acknowledged that it was the older people who used the milkman and who would miss the service now that it had been stopped. Being unable to have a milk delivery again may seem unimportant to some, but to Julie and Della, it was an example of something that they had been prevented from having because of their postcode, and also because of the poor design of the estate, and the association that the estate had to violent crime. They believed that the estate's physical appearance and structure 'bred crime'; as they argued, the 'rat runs' were dark and narrow, therefore making the estate an easy target for anyone wanting to commit crime, particularly relating to drug use and dealing.

This subject was always a complicated subject for all of the women I spoke to. Most were extremely angry and worried regarding the amount of drug dealing and drug using on the estate, which they felt was exacerbated by the poorly lit and narrow walkways. However, at the same time there was also a kind of acceptance that it was here on the estate, another part of the fabric of the estate, and many of the women had involvements weak and strong to the drug economy in St Ann's, because of friends, family members, neighbours, and sometimes even their own involvement. The 'drug economy' within the estate is a constant theme that this book returns to throughout the following chapters. The issue of drug dealing and drug using has been raised constantly throughout the eight years of my research, but it has been an issue on the estate from the early 1990s. It has reached into many aspects of the lives of the people who live on this estate, and also other similar neighbourhoods in Nottingham and throughout the UK.

Drug dealing on the estate can be openly seen and witnessed by anyone walking through the neighbourhood, if you know what you are looking for or at. As we walked through the estate canvassing for the election we saw drug users hanging around the 'rat runs', waiting for a taxi to pull up, and dealers getting out while the taxi was waiting at the end of the 'rat run'. You can see the 'shotters' (young drug runners) waiting on their allocated spots, usually outside corner shops, for their regular customers. It seems that with every corner shop on the estate that predominantly sells lottery tickets, electric cards, alcohol and cigarettes and very little else on the shelves inside the store, outside the shop you can buy heroin, cannabis, and crack cocaine. At the back of the derelict pubs, which were once the heart and soul of the estate, there are now old mattresses and bits of furniture that the drug users use when 'shooting up' (injecting heroin). There are also several houses on the estate that are known to be 'crack houses'. (A 'crack house' is someone's home that they either rent or, in some cases, have bought from the council, and the occupier either allows drug using and dealing to occur within the property or more likely, the occupier uses and deals drugs themselves, and allow others to use their home for the same purpose.) The problems caused by the drug economy in St Ann's were always prevalent, either through complaints about the problems it was causing or the lack of care and attention that the authorities gave to those problems, and sometimes through the women's own involvement, both weak and strong.

Picking up litter

During the summer of 2007 I became involved with another group of women on the estate who were trying to get a local park cleaned up, so it would be safe for the children to play in, and also so they could use it with their children, or to walk their dogs. The park was the only real green space on the estate, as the few children's play areas dotted around within the rows of houses are also grey, gravelled and concrete. During the 1960s and 1970s the park had tennis courts and a bowling green, and there was also a scout hut on the site. Over the last 15 years it had fallen into disrepair, and the full-time park keepers were made redundant towards the end of the 1980s; the scout hut was abandoned at about the same time. Like many of the abandoned spaces on the estate, drug users and prostitutes now used it. Over that summer several tents had appeared, and the park was becoming a place for the homeless to live. The park backs on to a popular youth club and community centre, and some of the young people who attended the youth club in the evenings engaged in a game they called 'brick the cat'. A 'cat' is a term that the local young people use to identify crack users, and often when drug users came to the park to 'score' (buy drugs), some of the young people from the youth club would throw stones and bricks at them. Therefore the park became an extremely unsafe place in the evenings because of the kerb crawlers and 'punters' that the drug users and prostitutes attracted, and it also became unsafe for the drug users, as the local children and young people regularly threw stones and bricks at them.

The group of local women who had come together to campaign for the park to be cleaned up and re-launched as a place for children and families were unhappy about the lack of safe areas for children to play in in the neighbourhood. Rona, a single mother of four girls, told me she thought that the neighbourhood itself had quite a lot for her children to do – they went to the youth clubs and the community centre – but she told me:

> "… there is quite a lot for kids to do in the area but the only thing that the kids are missing out on today is good old-fashioned parks."

Most of the mothers on this estate had told me the same thing, that the youth clubs and community centre for children and young people on the estate were well established and well attended, but there was a lack of 'safe' green spaces for their children and for themselves. Karen and Anne were young single mums in their twenties, and both lived in Karen's home on the estate – Anne had fallen out with some of her neighbours and so had moved into her friend Karen's house with her son and Karen's two sons. They were both anxious about letting their children out on the street to play:

> **ANNE:** "… yeah, the other day he [son] wanted to go on park to play football so I said right I'll come down with you and I went but I didn't tek [take] me fags with me or anything and I was gagging, I sat there as long as I could and I said come on then and he said 'one more game please' and I couldn't say no could I 'cos all the other kids were there and he was the only one being watched. I felt away when I had to take him and I thought well you know if the estate was different you could leave him but you can't risk it but I did feel quite sorry for him."

> **KAREN:** "… well I'm worried that the kids laugh at him [son] 'cos he has to go in and then he gets bullied more, but I worry about someone taking him but he is sensible but I worry that he might follow the bigger boys and then get lost and not know his way back."

Karen and Anne had both joined the group of women trying to clean up the park. There were about 10 women in total, and they met at the local community centre with the neighbourhood liaison officer who was employed by the city council. Two or three 'cleaning-up' sessions were organised throughout the school summer holidays in 2007, many families and children joined in with the council Street Scene Team, and eventually, at the end of August, a fun day was organised in the park. There was a sound system playing reggae and dancehall music, face painting, a football tournament, and food stalls. The event was well attended and lots of children and young people came along to take part. However, the upkeep and clean-up operation was not continued, either by the council or the residents, and very soon the park became the favourite spot for the drug users, and 'brick the cat' was again established as an unofficial past time for the young people at the youth club. There was another effort in the summer of 2008 to clean up the park, but this time the clean-up operation and getting residents interested and committed to the project failed.

Although the residents in St Ann's remembered how this park was once well kept, recent attempts to clean it up amounted to picking up litter, cutting the abandoned grassy areas, and asking residents to raise money for the fun day.

It is often presumed that there is availability to all regarding the services and facilities that large modern cities in the UK have at their disposal. However, issues of access, location and exclusion within poor inner-city neighbourhoods are different to those of the large council estates at the fringes of a city, where social exclusion is seen to be actual and physical exclusion of their residents. It might appear that those who live in St Ann's, because of the close proximity to the city, have reasonable access to social and cultural products within the city centre, but even though the estate is in central Nottingham and it is not physically difficult to get to the city centre, residents still don't use the cultural and leisure facilities that on offer. In fact, the women and their families in St Ann's spend much of their time within the estate, and all of their time with friends, family, and neighbours on the estate, and are equally as excluded from the services and leisure activities of the city centre as those living on the outer city council estates. This makes what happens to and within the estate extremely important – local issues and problems within a poor neighbourhood are felt sharply by those within them, having an impact on what they do, how they think, shaping how they see the world and themselves.

It is therefore very common on this estate, and not at all unusual, that the women are involved in community projects, often voluntarily or unofficially; very rarely officially and paid. Many of the initiatives that were set up in order to deal effectively with the problems in St Ann's have largely been centred on skills and training to prepare residents for employment, to change local neighbourhood practices, and to improve parenting skills. There are groups of women in St Ann's who are working, sometimes part time and more often voluntarily within the community on community projects. Unfortunately many of these projects are ill thought out, very short term, with no real commitment to them, and so the apathy shown by the local authorities is often matched by the apathy of the local residents in response.

My description of the living space in 'St Ann's' is not unusual – there are many 1970s-built council housing estates up and down the UK that have come to be viewed as oppressive by the many who have been allocated housing on them, through the thoughtlessness and poor design of the estates rather than the population living within them. Even though the women accept and know that there are incidents on the estate that make life harder for all residents, there are those who try to make their living space better for themselves and for their families. Nevertheless, as one resident told me, "... living in St Ann's is like living at the bottom of a mountain; you are always waiting for the next avalanche". Therefore, for many of the residents, the difficulties they encounter are often absorbed into daily life and become part of what it means to live in St Ann's.

Rough and ready

The women understood and accepted that their neighbourhood had been associated with crime and poverty for generations. Some of the older women had known about the Coates and Silburn poverty study in the 1960s, and often discussed how this association was particularly stigmatising for St Ann's residents. The women I spoke to were especially aware of the media representation of the estate, and how badly the estate was thought of in wider Nottingham. I spoke to Mandy, a lifelong resident of St Ann's; she had lived on the estate as a child with her family, and now resided in St Ann's as mother to her own children. Over the last five years there had been a particular association with gun crime in the city of Nottingham. This representation was yet another issue the women had to face on a daily basis, their neighbourhood being represented as 'lawless', and unruly. As Mandy told me:

MANDY: "It's like people looking in, I mean it's when you've heard it on the telly about the gun crime and everything, I mean my friend she actually made a complaint the other year 'cos she went to a pantomime at the Nottingham Ice Stadium and one of the people in the pantomime, he turned round and said 'oh I don't want to go into St Ann's 'cos we'll get shot' and they brought that into the pantomime and my friend actually made a complaint about it."

LISA: "So they actually made a joke and other local people in the audience could laugh at it."

MANDY: "Yeah, but for us that's not funny."

As Mandy said, this was not funny to her – her whole family lived on the estate, she was raising her three children on the estate, and she told me she had known some of the young people and their families who have been victims of gun and knife crime. Therefore, for her, and for many of the women I spoke to, when jokes and nasty comments were made about the estate, it was often a painful and humiliating experience. When I visited Shirley, a mother of three grown-up children who had lived in St Ann's her whole life, her 18-year-old daughter Rachel joined in the discussion, particularly when we began to talk about how the estate was viewed from the outside:

RACHEL: "Well, if you're St Ann's, everyone thinks you're like scary and people say to me 'Where you from?' and I say St Ann's and people are like [gasp] and I'm like, it's not that bad; they think everyone round here is gangsters, it's only people who are not from here who think it."

SHIRLEY: "Yeah, I remember once was it last year I was up city hospital 'cos I was visiting a friend of mine who was terminally ill and I said ay yer [are you] gonna give us a lift and there was this other guy who was with another friend said oh 'where abouts do you live?' and I said St Ann's and he said you never are, are you giving her a lift down there? Will you be alright? And I

said 'yeah he'll be alright with me I'm a gangsteress' – the small
mindedness of some people it really gets to me.'"

These accounts of how 'others' had often spoken of St Ann's in
derogatory ways were common in the women's stories. All of the
women I spoke to had similar experiences when they often felt they
had to justify why they lived in St Ann's. As Rachel said, "It's not that
bad." However, all of the women I spoke to said that when you said
you were from St Ann's, it always provoked some kind of reaction,
and it was never a positive one.

Most of the women wanted to talk about the neighbourhood,
especially how it was being represented on the outside, but also how
they, as residents, and women, had been represented. Louise, like
many of the women I spoke to, had been raised on the estate; her
family had been given a house immediately after the slum clearance
programme in St Ann's. Louise's family had been one of the Irish
families that came to St Ann's in the 1950s, and they were extremely
proud of their 'new' house when the council handed the keys over
in 1970. Louise told me how her mum had thought that they were
'posh' in the brand new house, and tried to keep it immaculate despite
having five children. The whole family still lived in St Ann's within
a few streets of each other, but they did not feel so 'posh' and proud
of the estate now. As Louise told me:

> "When you tell people where you come from, yeah, you feel like
> you know that they class you like rough and ready."

Louise told me that not only were you considered "rough" because
of the notoriety of the estate, you were also "ready".

Being ready

'Being ready' meant that women from St Ann's were often represented
as 'slags', having little value apart from their sexuality. Many of the
women talked to me about how they were often viewed as women
who were 'easy' – "they think we have no morals". This overt
sexualised reading of the women in St Ann's was especially true

for those who took part in this research, as they understood their sexualised position, through being working-class women, council estate women, and also through their association with black men. All of the women with adult sons and daughters spoke about being thought of as 'slags or prostitutes' because they had mixed-race children. Even the younger women brought up this subject. One young mum who was 21 told me that she thought others, those who did not live in St Ann's, saw her as 'tainted' because of her mixed-race children. Shirley, whose eldest daughter was 30, explained that when she first started dating black men in the 1970s many of the women on the estate had warned her that "no white man will touch you now". Louise, who had said that people thought she "was rough and ready", also told me that when she had become pregnant with her daughter, now 28, her father had been particularly upset because she was the second of his daughters who had come home with a mixed-race baby. This was especially hard for him because he thought that he would be a "laughing stock" among other white Irish men because of the perceived promiscuity of his daughters.

There has been an ongoing debate regarding how white working-class women, when linked to poverty, have been objectified and sexualised (Skeggs, 1997). However, there is very little academic understanding of how the white women in this research are often demeaned and disrespected, not just because they are white and poor women living on council estates, but also because they have had sexual relationships with black men. Those women whose children were now adults remembered the 'looks' and the 'comments' that came from within the estate during the 1970s and early in the 1980s. When I met Claire, now 31, she described herself as a 'lifer' on St Ann's, and recounted a very early memory coming home from junior school with her best friend, a black boy of the same age:

"My first black friend was one of my closest friends at junior school, we were only about nine and he used to walk me home from school and we walked up the close and my mum was at the back door; she could see us walking up and she shouted me, and as we walked up she opened the gate and let the dog out to bite my friend and it bit his leg and then his mum came up and

I remember the beating I got for being a black man's lover and you know ... 'you little prostitute, what do you wanna go with them for? You're not having them as friends.' I was nine but me and my friend was tight and we were good friends and still to this day we are friends; we'll talk about what happened and I still feel sad for her behaviour to him."

This type of abuse that Claire had endured from her mother was regular and common within her family life. She had lived with this abuse until she left home when she was 13 to live with Shirley and her children on the next street. Shirley looked after her as one of her own children until Claire was 18 and the council gave her a flat on the estate. I found out that this practice was not uncommon on the estate among the older women – many of the women I spoke to had been taken in by other families, or had taken other children into their homes. However, for Claire, the abuse from her mother never stopped, even while she lived with Shirley. Her mother continued to call her a 'slag' and a prostitute because she was living with Shirley, whose children were mixed race, and the abuse continued when Claire had her own daughter, who is also mixed race.

Many of the older women I met told me that there had been a close association, particularly throughout the 1970s and 1980s, with white women who had black partners and prostitution, especially when those women lived on the St Ann's estate. This appeared to be a common and stigmatising association. I met Gaynor who had moved to St Ann's in the early 1980s from one of the mining towns in Nottinghamshire so she could be with her 'baby daddy', now her husband. Gaynor told me that the rumour in her home town was that she had 'gone to be a prostitute in Nottingham'. She told me that even her own family had believed it, when in actual fact, the first job she had secured when arriving in St Ann's in 1981 was as a dinner lady at the local school.

There has been very recent discussion in the public sphere relating to how the poor white working class have been subject to a 'racialising' of their position, from white to 'dirty white' (Haylett, 2001, p 355), and for the women in this research, their social positions were racialised because of their poor white working-class position, and also because they were mothers to non-white children, which both simultaneously sexualised and racialised their position. The complexities of these contemporary social positions for the white working class are difficult to unravel, but are important, if not central, to the women's understanding, and indeed, their process, of how they identify themselves. There are two issues here: first, the association of black men being 'sexual monsters', and second, an overt feminised version of white women in comparison. However, this feminised version of the white woman is not freely available to the women in St Ann's. Bev Skeggs' argument, that femininity is a cultural resource belonging to the middle class, is important. Consequently, it is the poor white working-class women who are not able to use it as a resource in gaining respectability. At the beginning of this chapter I noted that respectability is usually the first casualty for young working-class women. Hence they are positioned as the unrespectable very early on in their lives – their position in society is one of disrespect, and they have to work extremely hard to try and move themselves from this position, which they rarely do.

The white working-class women on this estate know that they are thought of as 'rough and ready', they understand this through what is known, and thought, about them; the way they act, where they live and who they share their beds with adds to this stigmatisation. This is especially true for those who have mixed-race children – for them, their cultural and sexual practices are exposed through what they do, where they live, how they look, and within their children's faces.

Even though all of the women I spoke to said that this type of association of white women being 'slags' or 'prostitutes' no longer happens within the estate, or rather from the estate's residents, I have come across many examples of those who do not live on the estate who still hold those stigmatising and racist understandings around interracial relationships, and the stigmatising association of being white and working class and a woman.

During the very early days of the research process I was waiting in one of the primary schools in St Ann's to meet the headteacher. The school secretary was chatting to me while I waited, and asked me what I was doing and where I had come from. I told her that I knew the headteacher and that my own son had attended this school previously, and that I was studying at the university researching white mothers with mixed-race children. The school secretary said she was happy that I was doing this research, and "it was about time someone did something about this problem", which she said, "was becoming worse". Initially I was unsure as to what the 'problem' was. I then understood that the problem was the increasing amount of mixed-race children who had white mothers attending school. The secretary went on to tell me that the children were emotionally unbalanced, and felt that this could lead to medical problems, as the same 'black men' were impregnating different white women, and interbreeding was the natural conclusion. This was only one of those situations where I heard first hand what others thought about my community, not realising that I am part of that estate and my family and friends are those people they are passing judgement upon.

All of the women had said that this common 'Nottingham knowledge', which positions the women from St Ann's as 'rough and ready', still exists outside of the estate, and they were regularly subject to this view. This was often given as the reason why some of the women had moved into St Ann's, but also why they stayed there. Their mixed-race children and interracial relationships were 'normal' and accepted within the St Ann's estate, and they were not made to feel that they had 'done something wrong', at least from those who lived there. Gina was 21 when I met her and she had two young sons. She had moved into St Ann's because of the racism she had experienced while living in another part of Nottingham, and also because of how she, as a white woman who had a black boyfriend, had been treated by her neighbours:

> "I was having a lot of racism letters through my door saying you wog lover ... this that and the other ... don't bring these black kids round here, I was having all that and then I got my windows smashed by some racist people."

Gina was grateful for the house in St Ann's because of the amount of women in the neighbourhood 'like her', and because of the amount of mixed-race children on the estate. She recognised her stigmatised position outside of the estate, which she understood had worsened when she became a St Ann's resident. However, she knew that being a young single mum whose children were mixed race was not perceived as being a negative 'by the rest of St Ann's'.

For the white women on this estate, being thought of as 'rough and ready' and a 'slag' may reveal a racist assumption that white women can only be attracted to black men because they are sexually promiscuous, often immoral, and deficient in some way. Their social positions, at least outside of the estate, are diminished by their non-white children – they become extremely visible, and in some parts of the UK, they have become a short-hand marker of how Britain's underclass now looks.

Being and belonging to St Ann's

As a consequence of devaluing an entire neighbourhood and its residents, It is hardly surprising that the neighbourhood itself was particularly valuable to its residents, given the stigma that they experience from those outside of the estate. 'Being St Ann's' meant a great deal to the women, and was very important to them. 'Being St Ann's', or 'when you're St Ann's' were phrases that many of the residents used about themselves and their families; 'we are typical St Ann's' was another common description. Some of the women I had spoken to had moved out of St Ann's at various times to other estates around the city, but all had moved back because, as Shirley told me:

> "I had total withdrawal symptoms and felt like a fish out of water
> so I come back to St Ann's."

When I asked Shirley what made St Ann's St Ann's, she told me it was about people:

> "It is a really nice community even though it has got a lot of bad
> press over the last few years, but again there's all different pots of
> the community – the old folks you know the next generation up,
> the old Brendas and the old Bills you know, who have watched
> you grow up and then there's people my age you know, who
> I've seen grow up; some of them might be drug dealers, some

are the local alcoholics or whatever, but there's all different pots
of the community, but faces are more important than places."

The women were proud of some aspects of their community despite
the problems they faced, and they spoke about the neighbourhood
fondly and with some gratitude, especially in the context of how
'others' represented them. Even when they discussed the negative
aspects of the neighbourhood (of which there are many), they
recounted the examples of 'badness' in a context that may be difficult
for many to understand. The neighbourhood, regardless of its
problems, represented home, community and also their place of safety.

During the New Labour years of government, the concept of
'social exclusion' was introduced and heavily invested in. However,
when I talked to the women about social exclusion, and explained
that St Ann's was considered a socially excluded neighbourhood and
that they themselves were also considered to be socially excluded,
some of the women thought this was quite funny, and laughed at
the idea that they had been classified in such a way. When I asked
Gina, a 21-year-old single mum, and her friend Zena, a 29-year-old
single mum, if they had heard of social exclusion, neither of them
had, and did not think the concept really applied to them, or rather
not from within their community:

> **GINA:** "Really ... no I'm not excluded I don't think I am ...
> but certain people who you talk to do, I suppose, exclude you
> a bit ... yer know, like when you ring up the council and I'm
> talking to them and because I'm on benefits ... well I don't think
> about myself as poor but I suppose I am poor, but it's people
> who judge me."

> **ZENA:** "Well I'm not socially excluded but people do look at
> me in a certain way ... with a certain idea in their mind like I'm
> a chav with loads of gold, do you mean that?"

All of the women, however, thought that they were being excluded in
the way they felt 'looked down on', and they thought that exclusion
was a process that happened to them by 'others', in a similar way to

how their children were often excluded from school. They felt that this exclusionary process was something they had no control over. As Zena said to me, she had no control over what was in someone else's mind when they saw her.

Some of the women in the research understood exclusion through material goods, things they could not afford, which they understood made them different to the rest of society – not being able to afford a new carpet when they needed it, or being aware that 'others' could. Gina told me that she did not really think of herself as 'poor' or 'excluded', although she knew that others did. She only recognised herself as excluded or poor whenever she came into contact with any of the benefit agencies. She felt that these 'labels' had been placed on her and she was judged because of them. She said that every time she gave her address to any of the officials she came into contact with, there was often a silence as they mentally processed her single-parent status, the ethnicity of her children, and then her address in St Ann's:

> "I know what they're thinking you can see it ticking over in their brain as you wait for them to think 'oh it's one of them from there.'"

When I met Lorraine she had agreed to speak to me only after she had found out whom I was related to, and spoke to other women about me 'to see if I was really one of them and could be trusted'. This was important to Lorraine because she had only recently ended a prison sentence of two-and-a-half years and was trying to rebuild her life with only two of her five children being returned to her from local authority care. Now in her early thirties, she had lived in St Ann's since being a baby when her mother came over from Ireland in the 1970s. We spoke about social exclusion because she had 'picked up' its meaning from the various social workers, health visitors, and solicitors she had been in contact with. Lorraine had a particular understanding of what exclusion meant for her, although she had an idea of the official meaning because she told me her barrister had used the definition in her mitigation at court. Two of her children were still in foster care in a well-known middle-class neighbourhood in another part of Nottingham. She had visited this affluent neighbourhood in order to see her children, and when I asked her about exclusion, she understood how she had been 'excluded' from having things that others had access to, and this included her own children:

> "Well you know it's the people from West Bridgford and that whose got a bit of money and bit better stuff in their house and they can afford to buy a bit better ... that shouldn't be nothing; anyway it shouldn't matter where people live and how much money they've got, we should all be equal, but living here in St Ann's, I know that's not how it is."

Lorraine also knew that by having 'a bit of money' and living in 'a respectable' neighbourhood, this not only allowed you to have "a bit better stuff", but also enabled you to be free from stigma and inequality. She understood the perceived differences between St Ann's and its residents, and other more affluent neighbourhoods and the people who lived in them. She had gained this awareness through social services, and social workers involved in her family who told her that her two children were 'safer' in this more affluent neighbourhood with their 'white foster parents' in this all-white neighbourhood, which Lorraine objected to:

> "The people who've got my children now who don't know nothing about black people; the social worker said the other day that they are sending someone down there to teach 'em about dual heritage kids and I was like, hold on, I'm here perfectly good to look after my kids, why are you paying someone to go down there and teach them about dual heritage? Let them look after the white kids and send mine home 'cos mine don't belong down there."

Lorraine felt that she was being 'excluded' from society by those 'who looked down on her' and who judged her because of her situation. She also argued that her children in foster care were being excluded from who they were, and where they belonged, which was mixed-race children from St Ann's. Although I am not asserting here that the social workers are wrong, and that Lorraine is right, the point is to show that 'belonging' was important for Lorraine. She felt 'looked down on' and excluded by those who she came into contact with from outside of the estate, and so belonging to the estate mattered all the more. Many of the women talked about 'being St Ann's' – St Ann's can mean both place and people, to those inside, as it does to those on the outside. This is the spatial element of exclusion – who can belong to society and who are 'the imperfect people', a class positioning of those who live on the margins of society, and who can be identified by the rest of the population (Sibley, 1994, p 69). However, these negative identifications also have meaning to those they are aimed at. It seems that once the 'excluded' are recognised and identified through their physical space, where they live, and the symbolic social space (in this case, the excluded space is gendered, racialised and sexualised), both spaces are subject to symbolic violence (Skeggs, 2004). Lorraine and Gina explained what 'social exclusion' felt like for them as they experienced it. What they told us was that being 'poor' was an aspect of exclusion – being disrespected and 'looked down on' were felt sharply, as was the removal of personal power and control.

This chapter has shown from the outset the problems that arise through the thoughtlessness of those who make decisions for the many. It is undoubtedly difficult to live on this estate, partly through its design, partly through past local government and national neglect for the place and the people, but mostly through the inequalities that thrive within British society, allowing certain groups to become disrespected and stigmatised. The residents have an acute awareness of how they are viewed from the outside, and that is a constant problem for them in many ways. They are not sure why they are disrespected so acutely; sometimes they argue that it is because the estate has an unfair and inaccurate bad reputation. Sometimes they think it might have something to do with their own actions, because they claim benefits, or are single mums, maybe because they have no money, or because they wear too much gold – they are often unsure. They think it might be a combination of all these things, in addition to the ethnicity of their children and their 'babyfathers' – it seems the women on the estate have been simultaneously racialised and sexualised because they are white and working class, they live on a council estate, and their children are mixed race. They are fearful of and complain about being misunderstood and misrepresented, leaving them feeling extremely angry. This has sometimes resulted in violence, fear and hostility, and at the same time, as one woman told me, "it just makes me weak". Imogen Tyler, in her recent work *Revolting subjects* (2013), shows clearly that there is a clear narrative within the British social structure that those who are considered the 'underclass' are known and imagined as a 'race' and not a class, and that poverty and disadvantage are not understood of as economic, political or even structural, but as 'genetic'; the poorest of the working class have been racialised, as humans who are deficit, and lacking in what the rest of the population have in order to become 'good citizens'.

Both men (as we will see in the next chapter) and women on the estate were clear about feeling powerless, and that their views are not heard; they feel disrespected and demeaned, misrepresented, and ignored, usually through being 'looked down on'. This notion of 'being looked down on' by 'others' was especially felt by the women, consequently allowing a shared experience and a common unity, an identity, explained through 'being St Ann's'. The estate offered some respite from constantly 'being looked down on', and 'never feeling good enough', although this in no way compensated for the problems they had on the inside of the estate or on the outside. There was a real feeling among the residents of St Ann's that they had been left behind and were, in actual fact, not wanted. They understood exclusion in a similar way to how their children had been excluded from school; however, they were not sure what they had done wrong. They suspected that it might have something to do with not having a good job, or having little education. However, they also believed that because they lived in St Ann's they were stigmatised, which is a contradiction in terms as they felt it offered respite from stigma at the same time. Therefore the estate, and belonging to the estate, had real value to residents here, even though simultaneously 'being St Ann's' also had a devaluing effect on the outside.

There is a real issue of mobility here – space is often known through who belongs in it, and who does not – therefore the experiences, and the process of identifying who you are and where you belong, allows a consideration of how language, ideas and practices, in addition to power relations and resources, shape how groups self-identify, how they understand their place in the world, where they belong and where they are not welcome. The fear of being 'looked down on' and treated badly often means that the talent, skills and knowledge held within council estates usually stays there, unknown and unrecognised beyond the neighbourhood. Networks are rarely made on the outside, and if residents choose to leave they hardly ever return and so their skills and networks are lost.

3

The missing men

Towards the end of my doctoral research, which had focused on the women of St Ann's estate, I began to speak about St Ann's and my research at conferences and workshops. I was always asked, 'Where are the men?' Although I had not consciously excluded them from the research, or from my findings, the fact remained that the men in St Ann's were missing. In trying to understand why they appeared to be missing, I thought about the connections the women and myself had with the men during the research process. When I visited the women's homes, if there were men in the house, they were always leaving – none of them ever wanted to stay around a group of women, talking about the community and family life in St Ann's. On very rare occasions, a visiting babyfather, or brother, or friend, might hang about out of curiosity. During the early years of my research I focused on the group of mothers using the local community centre as a meeting place, and women were well represented in the local services and at schools, but there were very few men in those community spaces.

The women were not overly concerned about these 'missing men'; the community centre, the schools, the housing office and the local precinct – these were their spaces, and the men had little involvement in their activities and daily lives. There were many reasons for their absence, some of which I knew at the time. Many of the men did not live with the women they had relationships with on a full-time basis because it made little economic sense to the family to have a man 'officially' living at the address who was unemployed or employed in unstable and very low-paid work. Sometimes the men were involved in an 'underground' criminal economy (which thrives in this neighbourhood), handling stolen goods, or drug dealing at various levels. Having a man full time in your home therefore often carried too much risk, and the women told me that they did not want the police 'kicking down the door' looking for whoever, or whatever, putting their tenancy at risk, as it was usually the women who held the tenancies for the houses on the estate. In addition, these men had an occupational hazard of going to jail and were thus unreliable as full-time partners. Therefore when I met with the women in their homes, or in the community centre, the men were always leaving, on their way out, passing by, or just absent.

I won a Leverhulme Fellowship in 2010 that allowed me a further two years to continue the my ethnographic research on the estate. I decided to focus on the 'missing men of St Ann's'. So my search for the 'missing' St Ann's men began.

Finding the missing men

In actual fact, finding the men of St Ann's was relatively easy. They were in the gym, in the barbers shop, and quite often, in each other's flats. They were the babyfathers, brothers, boyfriends, and older sons of the women from the community centre, and so they were not difficult to track down. They were in and around the estate as regularly as the women, only in different spaces.

The main site of my interactions with the men was at the gym; it is on the edge of the estate, very close to the Victorian market area of the city, and was housed in what had previously been a fruit and vegetable wholesale warehouse. This part of Nottingham had a very long history as a busy and vibrant place. Until the early 1990s the area had warehoused fruit, vegetables, meat and fish, and there had been a very busy outdoor market on the site; many generations of St Ann's families had connections to the market. During the early 1990s the area fell into serious decline, as the warehouses closed; most then became derelict, and the area was then used mainly by street drinkers. The red-brick Victorian bath and wash house, which had been featured in the original Coates and Silburn 1960s study, was also situated in the marketplace. Although it had been updated in the 1970s with a swimming pool and a small fitness area, it still had the original Victorian Turkish baths and sauna. It has since been updated again, but during 2011 it was closed – all of the original Victorian features were demolished, leaving only the front of the building, and the marketplace was repaved and a water feature installed as an attempt to regenerate the area. This has caused mixed reactions – although the area was in serious decline, the outdoor market had been reduced to only one fruit and veg stall. The stallholder's family had been on this market for many generations, and was probably the last of the many market trading families from St Ann's still doing the markets.

The gym was in one of the old fruit and veg warehouses; it was a very large space, and had room inside for a full-size boxing ring, a mixed martial arts cage, a soft matted area for wrestling and grappling, and an area for 'bag work'. There was also a large space for free weights and gym equipment. After the market area regeneration, rents were raised considerably, and the gym moved in 2012 to a nearby empty building, which had once been a textile factory. I joined the gym at the end of 2009 and went almost every day for three years (I am still a member and am still part of the gym community). The gym is owned and run privately by two local men, and is what you might call a 'spit and sawdust' place – no frills and very basic amenities. It is relatively cheap to train at the gym, £15 a month or £7 a week, no administration or membership fees, and no contracts; there are consequently very few women in the gym as the facilities are quite basic. However, it is popular and very busy, and it also has a very good reputation as a place where men can train seriously – as they say in the gym, 'it's not for pussies'. The few women who do go to the gym, including me, have a laugh about the facilities – cold showers, no hairdryers, actually no electricity, and free sexual harassment. This is not entirely true, however – mostly the men in the gym are polite and pleasant. They do 'try it on' now and again, but mostly they just ignore you. Nonetheless, if you train hard and are tenacious, sticking with it, even when it gets hard, you will win the respect and friendship of the men. And this is the rule for everyone at the gym – it is serious place, almost a place of work, and it is definitely 'their' space. Some of the men are in there for four or five hours a day, working out and talking, mainly about football, training techniques, nutrition, boxing matches, and mixed martial arts fights. There is always plenty of gossip, especially on a Monday morning, as some of the men training in the gym 'work the doors' (security guards/staff on pubs and clubs in the city). You can always find out what has happened in the city during the weekend – if there have been any fights, stabbings, shootings, if anyone has been arrested, and who has been arguing with their girlfriends. This type of gym is an ethnographer's paradise, and compared to the initial guardedness of the women, I was quite taken aback by the openness of the men, a situation I had not expected.

Although I did not initially have any strong connections in the gym, I knew some of the men 'by sight', meaning that I had seen them around the estate, although they soon found out who I was. Within a few weeks, they began to talk to me quite openly. They found out the information they needed about me within the estate and then approached me, asking me specific questions. 'The game' in the gym with the men was very different to the women in the community centre. The men found out who I was and who I was connected to on the estate without the long extended conversations I had had with the women. I quickly built up relationships with the men in the gym, and after a while, I told them about my research, and they were really interested. Ever since, I have been engaged in conversations about the estate, what is happening in the news, local politics, national politics, and I am asked my views, and told their views, about many of these issues. I have often myself spent four or five hours in the gym gossiping, talking, arguing and working out.

Chatting business

Whenever I spoke to the men or women on the estate, we always talked about other people who lived on the estate – this is known as 'chatting business'. It is a common pastime in St Ann's, and is, in fact, an important part of 'being St Ann's': who is doing what with whom, and whose children are getting up to what and where, this is an important part of the community, it is how men and women in this community feel included: 'you've got to know what's going on' was often said to me in many different contexts. This was especially the case at the barbers, which is directly opposite the gym. It is a 'black barbers', meaning that it is owned and run by local black men, and the patrons are usually local black and mixed-race men; women also go in with their sons, usually after school. The barbers who work in the shop also train in the gym, and the men who go to the gym use the barbers. I initially visited the shop with my nephew to get his hair cut – he liked the patterns and swirls the barbers cut into his hair. I then began to visit, just to join in 'the chat'. Anyone who has visited a black barbers shop will know you can spend a substantial amount of time in there. There is no appointment system, you go in and wait your turn, which can take hours; this is part of the appeal. I think most men would be disappointed if they were quickly in and out. The men make the most of this time by discussing the same things they have discussed or will discuss in the gym – football, boxing, mixed martial arts, and current affairs – and again there is a lot of gossip. The shop is very noisy – voices are always raised when there are five men arguing about anything from football, to the 'yutes' (youths) on the estate; being as loud as possible is a necessity, and there is always lots of banter and "nuff joke".

I always found it a lively and friendly place. As the women usually went in after school with their children, during the day it was a very masculine space. The men never really minded me being there – they got used to me, as they did in the gym, and usually drew me into their conversations about politics and current affairs. They were interested in my opinions about politics and power, and were interested in what I thought about their opinions. I never really got involved with the football banter, although I did get to know what specific footballers were wearing, what cars they drove, and who they were going out with (the men talked about footballers in much the same way as some of the women might talk about celebrities). The men in the gym and in the barbers shop 'chatted business' probably more than the women had in the community centre. This 'chat' was central for the men to find out what was 'running' on the estate, who had gone to prison, who had split up from their partner, who had 'beef' (argument/conflict) with who. I began to realise that, just like the women, 'chatting business' for men was a crucial part of estate life. However, you also have to be 'chatted about' in order to be part of the community network, a position I know very well. This allowed me the access, the trust and the networks I had built up on the estate.

Over the years I have got to know many of the men very well, and I have built up a very strong picture of working-class life from the stories of the men living on a council estate in contemporary Britain. I have been invited to their homes, met their families, their children, their partners and wives, and I have discovered that 'being St Ann's' is equally as important to the men as it is to the women, perhaps even more so when you consider the estate represents identity, belonging, but also income.

After a few months of training in the gym, talking to the men as we trained, and watching them in the ring and in the cage, they began to 'take the piss' out of me, and dared me to get in the ring with them. Actually having watched them train, it did appeal to me, so I started training with Tony, now in his fifties, who started boxing at the YMCA when he was eight years old, turning professional in 1979. Tony had never known anything else but boxing; he had never worked outside of the sport, and now, as he was getting older and the sport had not left him with good health, he trained and shared his experience with men at the gym. Tony had come over to England from Jamaica during the 1960s; his parents had left him with relatives until he was six years old and then later sent for him and his brother, which was not uncommon for West Indian families during the 1960s. He arrived in St Ann's when it was the old back-to-back terraces.

He remembers being a small child in a big bed with his two other brothers which he shared until he left home at 17; he recalls being cold, and also having to fight. Tony talked about the old days growing up in St Ann's during the 1960s and 1970s, the strong Jamaican community – as a family they were very well connected to other Jamaican families on the estate – and he remembers lots of parties and social events. Tony also remembers it being tough, and the children were tough and always fighting. There were gangs of kids waiting around each corner, and at the ends of the alleys that ran down the backs of the old terraces. Most had their own bits of territory that they protected against others. This led Tony and his elder brother to start boxing at a young age, and they both then became professional fighters. Tony was a light welterweight and won the Commonwealth Championship in 1986. His brother won the European welterweight title and twice won the British welterweight title. Both brothers left Nottingham in the late 1970s to train in boxing clubs in London. Tony returned to St Ann's during the 1990s to look after his ageing mother after his father died. His elder brother, who had been a talented and well recognised sportsman, did not fare so well – his fall from grace has been well documented because of his addiction to drugs and alcohol (Jarratt, 2009).

Tony's brother returned to Nottingham for a while, but now lives in sheltered accommodation in another part of the country; he still visits his family, and occasionally comes down to the gym when he visits.

Tony spends most of his time at the gym, either training men on the pads, talking about boxing, or reminiscing about the old days and his fights of the past, his life in boxing. He has a strong philosophy of life which he attributes to his life in the ring and in the gym, and which he tries to pass on to the younger lads he trains. While he coaches boxing he also tries to impart knowledge about life. I often hear him shout at the lads, "Don't look out the ring there's nothing there", "concentrate on what you're doing, stay focused, if you're looking at other people you'll get hurt". I know the young lads he coaches are not aware that Tony is imparting lessons on life as well as boxing, but I do admire him for trying. Tony lives alone now, in a high-rise flat that he rents from the council close to the gym; he has children he sees rarely, but he visits his mother every day, he cooks for his family, and he has cooked for me – he prides himself on cooking Jamaican food and will cook and bring it in to the gym for people he likes. He is well known on the estate, well respected, and the gym and boxing is the centre of his world. Tony is not working, and claims benefits; he will probably never work again, and apart from boxing, he has no other work experience, and has been left in poor health. Does this mean that his contribution to his family, his community and society should not be valued? Tony's life experience and success as a boxer is a valuable asset to the local community – his knowledge is a valued resource, teaching younger men life skills through the art of boxing. But outside of the estate, he has little value – he has only known the boxing world, he has no cultural capital to trade his skills and knowledge in the open market, hence his value is local. But as the local is a devalued neighbourhood, consequently, he is also devalued.

In a place that has been institutionally devalued, these hubs of community such as the community centre for the women and the gym for the men are extremely important. They are places where people can meet each other, work out community networks, who belongs where, but also places where they are known, and where they can situate their own place in the community, that is, where they belong. Being known is such an important practice on this estate – it allows feelings of safety, community and shared identities, which lead to empathy and compassion.

This was as important to the men as it was to the women. Although the men at the gym and the barbers shop appeared to be less aware of others' opinions of them, they talked openly about how they made money, their time spent in jail, the problems they had had with the police in the neighbourhood, and their relationships with their girlfriends and babymothers. This frankness was surprising in contrast to the guardedness of the women, particularly when the men talked about drug dealing, and receiving and selling stolen goods. The women were constantly involved in local schools, Sure Start centres, community projects, housing offices, and benefit agencies – they knew they were being scrutinised and 'looked down on'; in contrast, the men had very little engagement with anyone from outside of the neighbourhood, and particularly with statutory services or projects, unless it was through the police and judicial system. They had minimum interaction with benefit agencies and housing departments, which amounted to signing on every two weeks in order to claim Jobseeker's Allowance, and some of the men did not do this, simply because they did not want to be connected to any address. They told me about the cat and mouse games they played with the police – they knew 'how to get around things'. If you had no address the police couldn't find you, and they needed substantial evidence to search an address you did not live at. The men spent most of their time with each other, and had strong friendships and family bonds, often introducing new friends to me as their 'cus' or their 'fam'; sometimes they were blood relatives, although mostly the family relationships were more complicated and interwoven within the estate. It was one of those things that if you had to ask how people were related, you were definitely an outsider. The networks, family ties and relationship to the estate were very important for both the men and women; 'being St Ann's' was the most likely way the women would describe themselves and their families, while the men subscribed to the idea that 'Stannz' was territory and belonged to them. I have met very few people who have imagined themselves 'being' or living anywhere else – moving out was not an ambition in this neighbourhood as a method of acknowledging social mobility and 'getting on in life', as Coates and Silburn discussed in their original study. Staying in the estate, belonging to it, and being respected and valued on the inside was always more important than leaving, and this was especially true for the men on the estate who, like the women, had found their own ways and methods of 'getting by'.

Although there were approximately 15 men who I got to know well over this two-year period, there were many more who had talked to me and told me their stories. Very few were in full-time stable employment – most worked in unstable or part-time employment. Nevertheless, they found ways to 'get by', although the difficulties relating to employment were always apparent. Chris was 24 when I met him. He was mixed race and his mother was white and lived on the estate. He worked as a self-employed barber at the barbers shop, although he trained at the gym most days, and was an amateur 'cage fighter'. He was one of the few lads in the gym who was working full time, and he had trained at a local college as a barber, and served an apprenticeship. He told me his motivation for going to college and doing an apprenticeship was watching all of his uncles go to jail, serving long sentences – his family had been part of an incident in the city relating to two rival gangs. He knew that he was 'lucky' only to be on the fringes rather than heavily involved. The training, and the camaraderie at the gym and the amateur fights he took part in and was often successful in, he attributed to not "getting into fuckery". Before Chris had trained as a barber he had found it difficult to get a job, and working as a self-employed barber in a black barbers shop offered him the opportunity to earn a living wage. Chris has no real formal education, and is close to his family and the local community; consequently he holds the same values and practices as those who visit the barbers shop. This makes him an asset in the local community – he knows the local styles, he knows the families and who is connected to whom, he speaks the same language, and gets involved in the banter. These cultural resources on the inside of the estate are not transferable, however – his language, the way he speaks and dresses, and his sense of humour would probably not transfer into a more mainstream salon in the city centre. Chris thought he was lucky to have this opportunity to work in his community, and with people like him, who he could have a laugh with, but he also knew how hard it was for his friends and family members to find jobs they felt as comfortable with.

Most of the men's lives did not have this rather heroic trajectory, of being able to train/work your way out of a bad situation; for most, their situation was far more precarious. Terry worked part time in his first job as a delivery driver for a supermarket. He was in his late thirties, and had served a long prison sentence as a teenager and into his twenties. He had managed to keep his head down doing 'runnings' (a Jamaican and local word meaning 'dealings', 'business') for a few years until he found employment as a delivery driver. Terry was one of the many men in the gym who was selling drugs – his business was cannabis, and he had a regular client base, that either picked up from his home, or he delivered to. Since starting his employment as a delivery driver he had found that he could manage both successfully, and the money he earned through both jobs meant he could afford the rent on a one-bedroom flat in St Ann's. Terry trained in the gym every day before or after his shift at work. He had a very tight circle of friends whom he had grown up with on the estate; he saw them regularly, and they kept in touch constantly through online gaming networks and BlackBerry Messenger (BBM). There were other men in the gym who had very similar lives to Terry; sometimes they worked in jobs part time, and had 'little runnings' on the side, and sometimes they had no official employment but 'hussled', which could mean anything from selling drugs, cannabis, steroids, Viagra, cocaine, crack, or heroin, and sometimes it was selling stolen goods (there was a healthy trade in sunglasses, glasses and leather jackets at the gym; one Christmas I bought two Waitrose organic corn-fed chickens). Many of the men claimed no welfare benefits, and effectively tried to stay off 'the system' altogether.

Consequently business is important to these men, and is talked about constantly. Stackzz was another regular in the gym. I remember him first training with Tony when he came out of jail. He had done a two-year sentence, and with a baby on the way, he really did not want to go back to jail. He was 27 when I first met him, and had been dealing drugs on the estate since he was 15, with intermittent jail sentences. He is cheeky, has a mouth full of gold teeth and scars on his face where he has been involved in fights with knives with rival dealers on different estates in the city. This time, however, he was determined to not go back to jail – he trains every day at the gym, and has competed in several amateur boxing matches, is ambitious and loves being in the ring. He has no formal education and has never had a 'proper job'. He is still dealing drugs, albeit in a much 'quieter' way, and has regular customers and is no longer involved with a gang. Preferring to live with his girlfriend and his child, the tenancy for their home is in his girlfriend's name, and like many of the men, he tries not to 'officially exist'; instead he 'gets by' with a much lower profile than he previously had. Stackzz is a great dad, and like most fathers, his aim is to provide for his child, although as 'officially' he does not live at the same address as his child and girlfriend, 'officially' he is absent, and 'officially' his girlfriend is a single parent.

The gym has become very important to Stackzz – his training, the fitness he now has and the friends he has made, as well as the goal of fighting and being involved in the amateur boxing scene. Stackzz says that this keeps him out of trouble, although many might think that his continued involvement in drug dealing means he is still in trouble. He earns what money he can through 'business', and his girlfriend has a part-time job. They live in social housing on the estate, close to both of their families and their friends. They are 'getting by' through their local networks, their part-time work, by claiming some welfare benefits and their runnings.

Passing by

I learned through attempting to track down the missing men in St Ann's that they are just as locally based as the women but they use different spaces and places on the estate. The women travelled around the estate, to the schools, community centres, various projects, and to the local services. However, the men, as I have stated, were not in any of those places. I had also noticed, or rather I hadn't, because It did not seem unusual, that when I visited the women's homes, the men who were living there or who were in relationships with the women, were either on their way out, or they were 'passing by'. I never really paid much attention to the 'passing by' life of the men until I began to work with them much more closely, and asked them about their lives. To 'pass by' is a term used by men on the estate to convey their plans for the day, and has its origins within the Jamaican community. It means to visit, but without any firm plans or commitment, so you might 'pass by' later. You can 'pass by' the gym, the barbers shop, your mum's house, your girlfriend's, or your babymother's house. However, 'passing by' also meant a lifestyle and a transient identity on the estate for the men.

Searching for these missing men was not as difficult as it might seem, as they were never far away and always on and around the estate, but in specific spaces rarely frequented by women and children; they were located in the community but in parallel spaces, at the gym, or in the barbers shop, and several of the men had their own flats where other male friends and relatives went and played Xbox (computer games). Xbox was also used to talk to each other, through playing games online, and the men were also in constant contact with each other through BBM. I began to know where and what the men did in a usual day, and also the transient life they lived. It was customary to let someone know you were about to 'pass by' usually through a text message, but more often through your BlackBerry, and it was actually very impolite to turn up unannounced. This practice was always about risk management – there was a lot of fear and suspicion on the estate, fear of the unannounced visitor, which meant the police, the 'social', the TV licensing people. It always meant problems, and doors would not be opened if they didn't know who was on the other side of it.

Both the men and the women's lives were full of practices of risk management, but in different ways. As I have discussed at some length, the women had an acute understanding of how they were known and 'looked down on'. Being a person of value is as important in St Ann's as it is for any group within society, and there was an overall consensus throughout the estate – and particularly within those families who had lived on council estates for several generations – that they were 'looked down on' and should feel ashamed of their council estate resident status, or worse, laughed at and ridiculed. The women focused on 'being St Ann's' as an identity and as a practice of 'belonging'. However, the men understood 'being St Ann's' as a process of territory, and this related to the estate and the space belonging to them as they 'passed by'.

Family life and value

Family and family life is extremely important in this neighbourhood, and the family and the idea of family is far from 'broken', as the political discourse and 'broken' Britain rhetoric would have us believe, although family life works in a different way in order to overcome the many barriers, hurdles and difficulties that structural and structuring inequality brings to poorer neighbourhoods. Council estates are complex, and so is family life within it. Consequently, what is valued and of value within the estate is also of a complex nature, although it is often simplified and misrecognised in order to fit with the discourses of the 'underclass' or the 'excluded' or 'broken' Britain. For women, a high value is placed on motherhood, and therefore being a mother ranks highly on the estate. Indeed, being a mother and coping with the difficulties of living on the estate are often the only things the women cite as being proud of in their lives, as well as being 'a mother' and a 'sufferer' (another Jamaican term that is widely used on the estate to describe endured hardships, even though being a 'sufferer' and enduring those hardships are always listed as personal achievements). During a discussion about the drug dealing on the estate with some of the men involved in the research, the discussion turned to how difficult life was for those who were part of the drug and gang culture. What follows is a discussion between Della, a white single mother of five children, Dread, her partner, a black African-Caribbean man in his forties who spends his time between Della's council house and a flat he rents in the neighbourhood, and Raphel, Della's eldest son, mixed race and 18 years old, who lives between his mum's house and his grandma's house, both on the estate.

> **RAPHEL:** "Boy, it's tough out there, man's killing man, you have to be ready, it's not easy to live in Notts, especially when you are Stannz [St Ann's], dem man out there wouldn't survive in here."

> **DREAD:** "Yeah, but … if you're gonna die for Nottingham die for Nottingham not just NG3 die for NG, that would make life a lot easier if that's what you want, just be NG, there's enough crackheads here for all of you to sell drugs to them, let's be honest about it here … there's enough crackheads for all of you to make money rather than dying, let's be honest … killing each other doesn't make sense, life's hard enough here, just do your business and done."

> **DELLA:** 'Well I try not to beat myself up about it anymore, I'm proud that my son breathes today, that's it, the way he is he does things which aren't legal but he makes money and he's still alive for now."

This discussion went on to describe the difficulties that Della, Dread and Raphel had in maintaining a family relationship amidst the problems on the estate. Della could not afford Dread to live with her full time, but they wanted to maintain a relationship, and Raphel struggled with his mum's relationship with Dread; there were also four other children living at home, and Della could not risk Raphel permanently living at the address because of his involvement with gang-related drug dealing on the estate. However, she was proud of her son as he was independent, he made money and sometimes helped her out, and more importantly, he was valued on the estate and was respected.

Because of the disappointments and difficulties working-class family life endures, there was often anger bubbling under the surface within this community. However, in the eight-year period of my research there has been a definite and progressive affect of despair, which can explode instantly and without warning into anger and situations of violence within the estate and between residents. The hopelessness and the feelings of constant hard work in order to get through any day was recounted by both the men and the women. The women described their lives as 'fighting brick walls', no one listening or caring about any of the problems they had. Della was having problems with her eldest daughter who was 14 and was truanting from school – although she was trying to keep her daughter in school, she said that she felt exhausted by what she described as the 'constant process'.

> "It's like fighting a brick wall; they hide behind policies like now if your child don't go to school you get a fine ... I've had a fine for my daughter for not going to school even though she was made to go to school every day. What she does, once she's up there isn't my fault so why should we get the fine?"

The women were also disappointed by services coming in and setting up projects offering 'false hope' of training and jobs, usually by offering voluntary work on the project. These projects often then retreated as quickly as they entered the community when funding ran out or when they realised the promises they made could not be realised. The men talked about the hopelessness of ever getting a job that offered economic stability and respect among their friends and family; they knew that getting a low-skilled, low-paid job would not give them a valued identity they needed to live on this estate, or even the means to live as 'a proper family', which was usually more of an aspiration for the future than a reality in the present. When I spoke to Dread about working and getting a job, his reaction was typical of many of the men on the estate:

> "There's no jobs here for anyone, what can I do now, I used to work for the council as a gardener, I liked that but that's gone now, I'm not doing no gay job in a call centre."

Robert MacDonald et al (2005) have used the term 'displaced masculinities' to describe the disengagement and difficulties young working-class men encounter in the transition from youth to adulthood, with the absence of 'masculine employment' offering status and respect. In this neighbourhood, status and respect are important resources, and to look for employment that may diminish local respect and status carries far too much risk and too much loss.

Misha and Tyler

I met Tyler in 2009. He was in the gym on the estate; he was cheeky, upfront and appeared very confident as he confronted me:

> "Yo, are you are fed [police]? What you taking photos in here for? … it's a gym, and you better not get my face on it, don't want feds in here."

Tyler was in the boxing ring at the back of gym working on the pads with Tony. They both stopped to see what I was doing – they couldn't resist as they had to know, and shouted me over, "Yo gal what you doing?" I went over to them with my camera. Tony knew me and introduced me as 'his friend Lisa', assuring Tyler that I was all right and that I lived on the estate, and that I was really clever and did something at the university. Tyler was immediately hooked by the word 'university':

> "University … university … I could go there … I might go there."

Tyler's interest, curiosity and initial sense of confidence was a pretty usual response to me, one of only three women training in the gym, and the only woman taking photos and spending large parts of my day in there among the men.

After his training session, Tyler came over and wanted to know more about what I was doing. He came to talk to me every day – he wanted to know everything about the university, what was it like? What were the people like? Were they nice to me? And what did they think of me coming from St Ann's? After a few weeks he invited me to his house, as he wanted me to meet his wife. I said I would go only if she invited me – I know the etiquette about men meeting women in gyms and that it can sound a bit dodgy. I was invited and visited. So I met Tyler's wife, Misha, who was 23, and both of them told me how they had met. Misha had come from Leicester as a student to Nottingham Trent University and was staying in student flats on the edge of St Ann's. Tyler had used his cheek and local charm to chat her up. It worked, and Misha was pregnant a few months after they started going out; they married, it was what they both wanted, and their little boy was born. Misha took a year out of university and went back when the baby was six months old to finish her degree. Tyler and Misha were devoted to each other, and Tyler wanted to be the best husband and father he could be. Although their time together had not been easy (Misha's family are Indian Sikh and Tyler is African-Caribbean), there had been difficulties with Misha's family because she had become pregnant, and had to suspend her degree, and had married a young black working-class man from St Ann's. However, they were overcoming these difficulties. Misha was also finding it hard living away from her family, and in St Ann's, where she didn't know many people, although they seemed very happy together.

Tyler, like many young men on the estate, had been involved in various 'runnings'; however, unlike many of his friends, he had left that behind, and was trying to set up his own business. He had a real ability to use computers and write programmes – he was completely self-taught, and he wanted to set up a social enterprise, teaching children to write their own computer games rather than play them. He had no qualifications but he had an infectious curiosity for everything. I continued to meet up with Tyler and saw Misha often with the baby – she was hoping to train as a teacher when the baby was a little older. Tyler was determined he was going to university, and he wanted to go to the University of Nottingham. Why? Because he knew that people like him and me found it difficult to get in there. I tried to tell him how difficult it was, and that the other students on his degree course would be very different to him, but he wanted it.

I didn't see Tyler for a few months, and then he contacted me and wanted to meet up. He was on a course and he wanted to find out how to apply to the university. I contacted the Widening Participation team at the University of Nottingham and the mature student officer met Tyler, and invited him to an open day. He was so excited and wanted this more than ever, but the course he had been on did not give him enough credits and was not enough to get him in. He was devastated. I suggested that he go to an alternative university, as there were others that were willing to accept him. I didn't hear from Tyler for a few more months and he wasn't in the gym. When I bumped into him in the city, he was really pleased to see me, and I was pleased to see him, but the first thing he said to me was, "Have you heard about me? Something mad has happened to me." I hadn't heard anything about him, although I had asked Tony at the gym where he was. I thought, 'oh no, what has he done?' I hoped he had not been arrested or got involved with his old friends, but what he said was far worse.

Misha and Tyler's baby boy had died of meningitis, when he was almost two years old. They were devastated and so was everyone who knew this young couple, as they had already been through so much. Misha and Tyler have since had another baby boy and are still as devoted to each other and their sons as they ever were. Despite how difficult their lives have been over the last two years, Tyler never gave up. He enrolled on an Access course, still determined to go to the University of Nottingham, but half-way through the year he was told that the university would not accept the Access course as he also needed a maths A-level at grade A or A★. You would think this young couple living in St Ann's, with the worst personal hardships to endure in their young married life, would have given up, and who could blame them? But Tyler did the maths A-level in his spare time – he used books and lectures on YouTube and attended the Access course at the same time. Tyler passed the course, and passed the maths A-level, but he got a grade B. The University of Nottingham decided to give him a chance despite the B grade. Misha would like to teach adult literacy in the community and is looking for some volunteer hours in St Ann's to help her to get on a teaching course for adult literacy at Nottingham Trent University. Tyler has just enrolled at the University of Nottingham and is in his first week of lectures. He is so proud of himself, and regularly posts pictures of himself on Facebook, sitting in lectures, in his University of Nottingham sweatshirt, but he often messages me, and tells me about the difficulties he encounters. I recently asked him how he was finding university life. He is doing brilliantly in class, and his studies are going well, but he is struggling with 'feeling out of place'. I told him to keep his head up as he has more than earned the right to be there, but still, as he said:

> "It makes me feel like I am a real common ghetto scumbag to the maximum."

Tyler feels 'out of place' at the University of Nottingham because he is a black working-class man, in a white middle-class space. Although there is no question that he has earned the right to be there, he recognises that his fellow students are different in the way they feel 'entitled' to their position and place, while he feels that he is 'lucky' and has been 'given a chance'. This is how Pierre Bourdieu's theoretical tools work in practice – violence is visited upon Tyler symbolically because he never recognises or is allowed to know his own worth.

The last I heard from Tyler was:

> "Yo, Lisa, how are you? My studies are going well, but I feel so out of place."

Unintended consequences

During the mid-2000s it became clear in St Ann's that most families did not consider that things might get better – 'just managing' was okay as long as the neighbourhood provided friends, family, and local value. However, since the end of 2010, apathy has been replaced by fear that things are getting worse, and that no one cares, that it is state policy to purposefully run down council estates, and their residents, through death, prison, or both. While the women attempt to work together for safety and support, the men are disconnected and further disconnect through their belief that they are 'on their own', and making as much money as possible by any means is their only route away from their situation. I say 'away' and not 'out' because there is no appetite to 'get out' of the neighbourhood: the goal is to stay within the neighbourhood and be successful according to the rules of the local value system, the logic being that being 'somebody' on the estate is always preferable to being 'nobody' on the outside. As some of the younger male respondents told me, "it's all about money, nothing else matters; if you have got money, no one cares who you are". They looked up to some of the older men on the estate, those with the nice cars, nice trainers; they recognised the respect and status that came with this local position. During a conversation in the boxing gym, a group of men explained to me the problems they had in getting jobs and earning money. They talked about the conspiracy theories they had read on the internet, and swapped information about new sites with 'new evidence', which, for them, explained 'their situation'. The most popular and talked about theory was that of the Illuminati, apparently an organisation that is centred round Jewish bankers and Zionist politics, which holds politicians, the media, the legal system and the banks in their hands. According to this theory, the Illuminati are part of the Masonic order, and their racism towards black people is purposeful and political, with the aim of keeping racial order and continuing inequality, thus keeping poor people in poverty, while its members and the Masonic order become more wealthy and more powerful. This theory is very popular among the men in the gym and the barbers shop. They talk about it constantly, and find different articles about it on the internet. There are many websites, and YouTube films the men cite within their arguments. They are especially interested in how the Illuminati apparently infiltrate and control American hip-hop music. They have told me of the elaborate theories that relate to the American hip-hop artist and rapper Jay-Z, and his wife and pop star diva Beyoncé who, they believe, are puppets for the Zionists. There is great detail on the internet, and then discussed by the men in the gym and the barbers shop, about 'secret signs' hip-hop artists make on their album covers and hidden meanings in their songs which show their loyalty to the Illuminati and the Masonic order.

While these theories are discussed in the greatest detail, argued about, and the men enjoy the debates that come from new evidence they find on the internet, there is little interest and even less knowledge of national and local politics, apart from the consensus that all politicians, like the police, cannot and should not be trusted. On many occasions, particularly after the 2011 riots, I engaged in conversations with these men regarding political and social change – the men were uninterested and disconnected, having no knowledge of where they were situated politically within the UK apart from knowing they were powerless, and believing that discrimination and disadvantage was related to an all-encompassing world order.

In this vacuum created by the lack of political connections and the absence of communication between a marginalised and excluded group of people and a society from which they feel cast out, it is no wonder that relations with the police and other officials representing the state have become both important and confrontational. The council, the 'social' and social workers have always been mistrusted, but when these state representatives are moving out of working in poorer neighbourhoods, either through centralisation of bureaucracy, or through redundancy, and increasingly, as services close down through current austerity measures and cuts, it is the repressive force of the police that becomes the sole representative of the state.

I am not arguing that there is no reason for the police to have such a high presence in this neighbourhood – there are crack houses on the estate which are impossible to live close to for other residents, there is prostitution and drug dealing, and there have been incidents of stabbings and shootings linked to gang violence. Ann Curtis, a US criminologist during the 1980s, introduced the concept of slow rioting in the 1980s to explain the rise in violent crime within urban areas of the US, and especially when violent crime is committed by the local community on to the local community – in the US this is called black-on-black crime. Slow rioting is what happens in a neighbourhood when there is internal and internalised social decay, leading to mass school rejection compensated by street knowledge and unemployment, leading to street work; when a community or group are rejected by the wider population and become a devalued people, their source of pride and success becomes local and relies on the local value system. Crime, drug dealing and teenage pregnancy become accepted and provable ways of becoming successful. There has been a return to the imagery of the 'underclass', with council estates representing a modern version of Hogarth's Gin Lane, with the two main characters – the dangerous and violent gang member and the welfare-absorbing single mother. The discourse of the underclass and their lack of common societal values and morality, and their wilful self-destruction and self-destructive behaviour, begin to represent a real threat to British values and national life, curbed only through punitive measures. So, it can be argued that street crime is, in many ways, a form of slow rioting: by committing crime on your own streets you are less likely to be arrested than if you go into a city centre and damage or steal the things of those who are powerful; and it is possible that some crime has become the safer and private expression of protest against an individual's social position, powerlessness and location (Curtis, 1985, p 8). The underground criminal economy thrives in this neighbourhood, as it does in all neighbourhoods where there is a lack of employment linked to financial autonomy and self-respect. Long-term joblessness and the proliferation of low pay and part-time employment, the widening gap between rich and poor, and dissatisfaction and disillusionment with mainstream politics, has meant a build-up of internal and internalised social decay. Being valued on the inside of the estate – 'being someone' – is always better than being 'no one' on the outside.

Internal networks therefore become important, although these tight internal networks are misrecognised by those on the outside who see local networks and practices as 'deficit' and 'troubled'. The residents on the estate become both recognised and recognisable characters within this national narrative of 'underclass'. They are living through a period in history that is extremely unstable – they are vulnerable to the market, and rely on welfare benefits and the state to keep 'their heads just above water'. Although they have been devalued as useful members of society, they find value for themselves locally, and from their adversity they find an identity that is meaningful to them.

This structural instability has had massive consequences for family life. Both the men and women talked about their aspirations to one day live as a 'proper family', perhaps when they both gained stable employment, and when the council rehoused them. This assault on family life through the precariousness of the economy and housing policies that the poorest families in the UK have no control of is shocking and extremely sad. The families on this estate have to live with the stigmatising narrative that 'they' are 'problems' and it is 'their' lifestyle choice to live in separated family units, or to struggle constantly on the edge of poverty, when clearly, the personal stories in this chapter show that the men and women on this estate have deeply held values relating to community and family life, and do everything that is necessary in order to live together, even when that means breaking the law.

4

'A little bit of sugar'

As I recount the many stories and experiences I have been part of in St Ann's, I am aware that even in the short amount of time between undertaking the research and writing the book there has been a decline in the real value of people's incomes and standards of living in recent years, particularly for those in the bottom 10 per cent of British society. There are many reasons for this, such as rising food and energy prices, the halt in pay rises for the average worker, the loss of low-paid but reliable work in the public sector, and the more draconian changes during the current austerity measures in welfare benefits, including tax credits, housing benefits and disability payments. At the same time, however, the highest earners are seeing their income levels rise. A study from the High Pay Centre, a think tank set up in the wake of an inquiry into escalating executive pay, says that the nation has returned to levels of income inequality last seen in the 1930s, with the share of the national income going to the top 1 per cent more than doubling since 1979, to 14.5 per cent (Hirsch, 2013). Danny Dorling's book *Injustice* (2010) gets to the heart of why social inequality and social injustice persists, but also explains that when levels of inequality are this stark, there is always a devastating effect on society as whole. It becomes especially debilitating for those in the bottom 10 per cent as they become financially, and socially, excluded, eventually becoming culturally excluded, and finding it difficult to take part in the same society as everyone else.

The road to Wigan Pier (1962) is George Orwell's narrative account of working-class Britain during the 1930s, when levels of inequality were staggering. He raised contentious issues relating to how the poor spent their money and conducted their social lives. This is a debate that is still raging today in the pages of the daily tabloid newspapers and in the pseudo-documentary style television programmes about 'the poor'. There appears to be an obsession in the British media in knowing how the working class and the non-working working class spend their money, choose their clothing, how and what they eat, and how they speak. These debates usually and historically conclude that the working class and the non-working working class bring most of their misery on themselves through their bad practices and bad choices (see Welshman [2007] for historical arguments of the underclass). In recent times this has been exacerbated by pseudo/reality documentaries claiming to show how life 'really is' on many council estates up and down the UK. Channel 4 have been responsible for many of these programmes, with shows such as 'Skint', 'How to get a council house' and 'Welfare Britain 1945'; however, the BBC have also aired similar shows, such as 'We pay your benefits' and 'People like us'. What these programmes have done in particular is to focus on and draw attention to the behaviour, family life and daily practices of those who live on council estates. There seems to be a clear agenda by the programme makers that rather than providing a sensitive and complex understanding of the difficulties that life brings when you live on council estates, or if you are unemployed, or have low-paid and unstable work, the programmes are aimed at a type of fetishist fascination of looking 'at' the poor, who are shown as 'deficit', as being ignorant, uneducated and lacking in moral judgement. Rather than looking at the structures in society, instead the default position of what is thought of working-class people is that they have something missing, something wrong with them, and if their behaviour and culture were righted that would solve the situation.

This is not a new position that those in the media and 'the rest of society' have taken relating to the poorest communities within the UK. Orwell noted back in 1930 that when people live 'on the dole' for many years they grow used to it – 'although it remains unpleasant it ceases to be shameful' (2001 [1986] p 80). Orwell explains that after many years of living in poor conditions, and with little money:

> ... the old, independent, workhouse-fearing tradition is undermined, just as the ancient fear of debt is undermined by the hire-purchase system.

So you have whole populations settling down, as it were, accepting that unemployment is necessary and living on welfare is the option to working in unstable and low-paid employment.

Although I do not entirely agree with Orwell, that people who live in the poorest conditions and without the proper means to live a dignified life in whatever society they are in 'get used to it', I do agree that they should be admired because they have not 'spiritually gone to pieces' (2001 [1986] p 80). The men and women in St Ann's have often proudly stated that they are strong and resourceful, and the proof of their strength and resourcefulness is the very fact that they are who they are, and that they live where they live, although they are fully aware of how they are diminished and 'looked down on' because of who they are. This is a situation that has barely changed over a hundred years. In *The road to Wigan Pier* Orwell notes that in the 1930s one of the 'distasteful practices' being undertaken by the unemployed and the lowest earners was that of getting married. There was much debate within middle-class society, channelled through popular newspapers, that unemployed men were getting married when they had no right to, as they could neither afford a wife, a home, nor children. Orwell asks in the 1930s, and I ask today in 2014, that is it right, that people who face such instability must cease to have a family? And because you are poor, on low pay or unemployed, this does not mean you cease to be a human being.

There is no doubt that when there is unemployment and a history of low pay and instability in a community and in a home that families become impoverished, but the family system has not broken down. People 'make do', they 'get by', they make their lives tolerable by lowering their standards and by becoming increasingly connected to their local communities. Even in the 1930s Orwell recognised that the films and cheap clothes made a difference to working-class life: '... only the corner of a leaky bedroom to go home to; but in your new clothes you can stand on the street corner, indulging in a private daydream of yourself as Clarke Gable or Greta Garbo, which compensates you for a great deal'. Today we might say something similar: 'having swagger [good style, nice clothes] on the estate matters'.

Consequently, lowering your living standards does not necessarily mean cutting out luxuries, an attitude that the middle class have always found abhorrent.

Orwell brings our attention to an article he found in *The New Statesman*, in 1931, where a reader wrote in and asked:

> ... would it not be better if they [the working class] spent more money on wholesome things like oranges and wholemeal bread.... Saved on fuel and ate raw carrots.

Similar questions are being asked today. In October 2013, after the major energy suppliers in the UK raised their prices by 10 per cent, a spokesperson for the Prime Minister suggested that wearing a warm jumper indoors would be an answer to those struggling to heat their homes. And I suppose the answer is yes, it would be better to spend your money on good, wholesome food, save on the electric bill by undercooking it and wearing an extra jumper in the house.

But as George Orwell argued (and I will do the same):

> ... no ordinary human being is ever going to do such a thing. The ordinary human being would sooner starve than live on brown

bread and raw carrots. When you are unemployed, which is to say when you are underfed, harassed, bored, and miserable, you don't want to eat dull wholesome food. You want something a little bit 'tasty'. (2001 [1986], p 80)

You don't want to live in absolute hardship with no comfort. Struggling to make ends meet is endless misery, and, as Orwell surmised, lots of sugar in your tea and a warm fire goes some way to relieving, even if just for a minute, the endless misery.

Gucci sunglasses

I have always felt uneasy regarding what I tell about this community, not least because I live there, and the people who I live among are friends, neighbours and family. But there is also something more fundamental to my working-class family life, and that is, the notion of 'washing your dirty linen in public'. This is a common analogy in working-class communities, and something I have been brought up with. It is an extremely important rule among working-class families, and especially for women. When you know and are fully aware that 'others' think you are rough, no good and valueless, the last thing you do is confirm this through admitting or allowing others to see your foibles. This puts immense pressure particularly on women when you have to 'tell' others of your poverty, misery or depression in order to 'get by', whether that is claiming welfare benefits, or trying to get support or help with anything ranging from your children's education to asking your GP for help when times are especially tough, by giving you a sick note so you can have some time off from your job, or asking for medication. This is always countered and balanced with the idea that you really should not be hanging out your 'dirty washing' in public, or, in other words, compounding the stereotype you live with from any self-admittance. Unfortunately, for the women on this estate, losing dignity is a very early casualty in 'getting by'.

Washing your dirty linen in public has not only applied to my personal life, but also regarding this research. What can I tell, what should I tell, and what damage will I do to people I care about and live among? I have wrestled constantly with the thoughts that by 'telling' my stories and the narratives from the inside, they may be used to compound the misery, unhappiness and difficult lives of the people in this research and this neighbourhood, and also those who live in similar neighbourhoods and who have similar lives throughout the UK. It has been tough, but I realise that if I am to speak from the 'inside', a position I have vehemently argued for, the voice of a working class-woman who has lived and grown up on council estates her whole life is needed in academia, sociology and the wider public spheres. Consequently I have to 'tell' what happens on the inside, but more importantly, why, and how, and I have to ensure that the 'telling' is contextualised in the environment where local practice is formed and played out. This is why I detail the space of the neighbourhood, its history, and the personalities within it. The following story is one I have felt most uneasy about, because it could easily be read in the same context of the stigmatising and harmful discourse I have spoken about previously.

Ayesha, like most of the men and women on the estate, had very little formal secondary education; she became pregnant at a young age, and had spent all of her adult life as a mother, and on benefits. She was really struggling with being on benefits – she wanted a job but was having difficulty finding one, having no experience, skills or education, although she was very active in the community, working with other young mums, albeit on a voluntary basis.

I was in the gym one Thursday morning, and Ayesha was there. Although she was a local woman and mother, she hadn't been part of my initial research with the women on the estate, but she was part of the gym, and one of the few women I saw in the gym regularly. I got to know Ayesha really well over the three years of my research.

One morning I noted that Ayesha was really low; she said that she was sick of never having any money and was struggling to get her kids what they needed for school, and her home needed decorating, but she didn't have the money. As Ayesha told me how 'pissed off' she was, she asked me if I thought she was a 'bad mum'. She was not the only woman to ask me this – being a 'bad mum' was a constant fear for the women on the estate. When you are valued through motherhood, and you, in turn, value motherhood, it is important that you are a 'good mum', and that others see you as such. When

I asked Ayesha why I might think she was a bad mum, she told me that there was no food left in the house and that she didn't get her benefits until the next day, so her kids would have to have cereal for their tea (evening meal). I told her that I didn't think badly of her for that, and that I had had to eat cereal on Thursday nights when I was a kid, and my own son had had to do the same for the same reasons. We both agreed that it was just how it was sometimes, you ran out of money. Ayesha was clearly upset, and was at a really low point. She said she had absolutely had enough of having nothing, and struggling. This type of struggle wears you down; it is soul destroying, and until you have ever been at this point, it is difficult to understand how awful you feel, and how valueless you see yourself. Constantly having nothing, and being unable to afford the things that you think might make you and your children happy, and valued, is an immense strain. This is especially apparent when all around you, through the media, and through the very well-equipped and well-resourced spaces of consumerism – city centres filled with shops with expensive things you can't afford, adverts in magazines and on television sending out messages that to be someone you need certain consumer items – all displaying very effectively what you cannot have. You consequently become valued through what you do have, and are devalued when you cannot afford those consumer items, or when you get into debt trying to acquire those things that enable you to feel you are a good and valued citizen, in a consumer-led society. Ayesha was caught in this trap. She felt utterly weighed down by the constant fear of running out of money, and having to go to a food bank. As a working-class woman, being unable to provide for your children and having to ask for a referral to a food bank is the ultimate disgrace; admitting defeat is most mothers' worst fear. I have known women who have told me that they would rather 'go on the game' (become a prostitute) than go to a food bank.

The next day was Friday, and after dropping her kids off at school, Ayesha came into the gym. She had been paid and got her benefits and was looking forward to going shopping and getting the kids some food. One of the guys came into the gym who sold sunglasses. He had a new selection of really good designer ones, and everyone was interested in having a look. He wanted £25 for each pair (they would probably sell in the shops for well over £100). Ayesha tried on a pair of Gucci sunglasses. They suited her and she looked great. I think she needed them – her mood changed, and many of the men told her how good she looked in them. So she bought them, at £25. Ayesha was really proud of those sunglasses – she told me she had lots of compliments when she wore them, and for months recounted the stories of her friends commenting on her good taste.

The reason I have struggled with this story is because it plays into the hands of those who think that living on benefits is an easy option, or a lifestyle choice. I have had sleepless nights while writing this book, worrying about what the *Daily Mail* or the Centre for Social Justice (the think tank set up by the Conservative Party), or Iain Duncan-Smith would use these stories for. However, this is an important story of council estate life. Those who live on council estates are often accused of having big television sets, state-of-the-art smart phones, expensive clothing, and that they spend their money (or rather, as 'they' see it, the state's money) on frivolity. Anyone who has ever had to live for any extended amount of time with very little knows how weary you become. You see others' lifestyles around you and through the media, and you are not allowed to join in. You live in a society that values high-branded and designer items such as Gucci, BlackBerry and Apple, but you are financially excluded from joining in. You are devalued for who you are and where you live, and like anyone else, you want to feel good about yourself. You want to be valued. Being valued outside of the estate is difficult, and I have explained in detail in previous chapters just how difficult this can be. However, being valued inside the estate is achievable, and for Ayesha, the Gucci sunglasses gave her value, but also a bit of comfort – they were the bit of sugar in her tea.

'Whatever they think I am, I am'

Knowing what other people think of you, those outside the estate, is one thing; I have talked about 'washing your dirty linen in public' and compounding negative stereotypes with your own actions, even when those actions are done out of necessity. However, there is also an acute understanding of what is known – or is thought to be known – about you by those on the inside. I often asked the men and women on the estate who they thought lived alongside them, who else resided on the estate.

Karen and Anne lived together with their children because Anne had fallen out with her neighbours, coincidentally, 'for chatting her business'. When I asked them one day, in Karen's kitchen, who lived in the neighbourhood, they told me:

> **KAREN:** "Tramps … [laughing].... Single mothers like me who have got no ambition and don't want to do anything with their lives and sit down and smoke weed and fags."

> **ANNE:** "Yeah, sit there all day chuffing … cup of tea … ashtray that's it, telly on [laughing] … and the kids being told to fuck off out the front door."

This conversation shows their awareness of the stigmatised view of women who live in St Ann's, and they play with the irony of their own situation, laughing at what they think others think of them, but also laughing at the women who they think this contempt is really aimed at. As they told me, they knew women on their street who were like this:

> **KAREN:** "Yeah, that's what you see."

> **ANNE:** "And what you know, you know people round here."

> **KAREN:** "From here to the bottom of the street, how many do you think goes to work?"

> **ANNE:** "Three probably, not many full time; there are some older women, a few that work."

> **KAREN:** "Well, when I was going to go to work full time when I just had [son's name] I was thinking, why should I go to work and slog my guts out when everyone else round here will have

a better life than me and I'll be tired at the end of the day, but
you have to force yourself to do it and rise above it."

The women in St Ann's understand exclusion and especially how
exclusion was felt from the real or imagined stigma from the view
of the 'other', the 'other' being those who lived in more affluent
neighbourhoods in Nottingham.

I also examined how hostility could be both externalised and
internalised, how those signifying systems of welfare and exclusion
can define a group but also influence how that group then sees itself.
There are external markers of living in St Ann's, how you dress and
look, and for the women, having your mixed-race children with you
allows you to be identified by 'others'; however, these identifications
are also internalised. In St Ann's it is the self which has absorbed those
negative signifying meanings of needing welfare provision, 'being
looked on', and being white, working class and mothers to
non-white children. Living in St Ann's is not simply an address to the
women on the estate; it has cultural and social meanings. The way
the women identify themselves is fraught with conflict, which takes
constant negotiation, often battling against the negativity about the
estate from the outside, but also by attaching themselves to what they
value on the inside by 'being St Ann's'. Their relationship with the
neighbourhood is complex: it offers some protection – it has valuable
services that the women particularly relate to St Ann's, for example,
the primary schools. The value attached to the primary schools is
because they *are* in St Ann's – they believe that their children are
getting something valuable because of the cultural make-up of the
neighbourhood. As the women say, "there are loads of mixed families
here", and this is important to them. However, there is another part to
this relationship that the women are fully aware of, that is, the negative
stereotypes of the estate, the racialised and sexualised perceptions of
women who live on the estate, and they balance all of these social
and cultural meanings, absorbing them into who they are, and how
they want to be seen, but also in what they do.

Those negative namings, feelings of 'being looked down on',
anger and humiliation, are absorbed into the self but can also act as
signifying systems to push against. Karen says that she 'forces herself

to rise above' what she imagines is expected of her, and also what she sees other women on the estate engaging in or not, especially when it comes to employment. The women on this estate do resist and adapt; they push against those negative stereotypes, although their resistance may not be obvious and is often misrecognised.

Julie, who was 38, and has two children (the eldest was 15 and mixed race and her youngest was eight and white) was one of the angriest people I met on the estate. The first time I met her she almost shouted at me for three hours about her frustration because of being unemployed and a single mother on the estate. She was aware how the outside saw people on the inside in St Ann's, and also understood why this might be:

> "Well, when I went to college after failing my GCSEs I did an Access course where I did some sociology and learned about the nature or nurture debate. I believe it's what you're born into; if my mum had money and I was born into money I wouldn't be going around with all these little runts ... sorry, I don't mean to say it like that but that's how everyone else sees 'em ... but because I was born into an inner-city working-class family that's all I've known init ... if I'd known about degrees for this and that and how to learn ... you only have to go out of St Ann's to see that there's a different way of living out there."

I asked Julie to expand on what she meant 'by being born into money' and how this could change people's outcomes:

> "The case of being born into money, well that money had to come from somewhere to start with back back back back; them people must have worked fucking hard for what they've got now. That's how people get born into it and when that system of money has you got you into the system of education like the Nottingham Girls High School."

What she is saying here is that she believes in the 'common understanding' of the discourse of 'middle-class meritocracy'. The narrative behind this is that the middle class deserve their social advantages through merit alone, and those advantages go unseen and unquestioned; consequently, working-class meritocracy is about working-class disadvantages being visible and linked to visible behaviour (Sayer, 2005, pp 61-9). Julie believed that those who had money, or who were born into it, must have deserved their wealth and success even if it was through the hard work of an ancestor, while she saw her own apparent failure as hers alone. Social history and personal history are important, especially when examining how groups of people understand their lives, and even more so when one group is severely disadvantaged by where they live, what they do, but more importantly, by who they are. This is particularly true when 'who you are' relates to an 'embodied history', a term used in sociology to explain an internalised second nature, a way of learning to act, to behave, learning what to expect and what not to expect, but to know these things without remembering that we have learned them. One of the fundamental effects of an 'embodied history' or, as Pierre Bourdieu terms it, the 'habitus' (the socially produced self) being internalised, is that there becomes an understanding of a 'common-sense world' (Bourdieu, 1990, p 56). Therefore, what happens both *around* people and indeed *to* people becomes as if 'natural' – reproducing and reinforcing those social structures, negative stereotypes and other signifying systems all identify individuals and groups through their difference. I am not saying that everyone's future is determined and that these are 'predictions', but what I am trying to do is to show how power works, creating the illusion of 'natural disadvantage', allowing the disadvantaged to be and to feel responsible for the inequalities they experience.

The consequence of being stigmatised and marginalised to such an extent that you understand the advantages of others as their own merit, and your disadvantages as your penance, has obvious and hidden effects on a community. The men and women on this estate have a keen awareness of 'their inadequacies' and their shortcomings in wider society, so it makes sense to acknowledge the value in engaging in the local culture and local community. Being 'someone' on the estate is always preferable to being 'no one' on the outside, so being part of the neighbourhood, being known and fitting in are elements to becoming a person of value on the estate. In particular, there has been an exchange of culture between residents, noting that they are proud of their success in 'mixing' and 'everyone getting on'. While this type of 'cultural mixing' has often been associated with 'youth culture', in St Ann's it is not limited just to young people; it has become a hybrid and interchangeable culture that has grown throughout the whole community over a 50-year period of the West Indian and white working-class communities living side by side. Particular ways of speaking, that is, using words originating from Jamaica, and in dressing (gold jewellery and expensive branded sportswear) are important; how you cook and eat is also relevant to your value on the estate (rice and peas and chicken is cooked and eaten by most families). These are cultural signifiers and have all been noted as important to what 'being St Ann's' means, and who is valued on the estate. The Jamaican community and their culture in St Ann's have always held a great deal of respect, and Jamaican styles of dressing, speaking and cooking are popular throughout St Ann's, regardless of whether you have any 'real' connections to Jamaica.

Being a person of value

How value is attributed on the estate and who becomes valued is extremely complex and has a hierarchical network that is clear to those who live in St Ann's, but it is extremely complex for those who do not. Lorraine was one woman who did not like the new people in St Ann's – the Iraqis, or the Polish, or the Africans. However, this racialised element to 'being St Ann's' had a strong correlation with a specific and local culture, linked to both the white working class and the Jamaican residents.

I met a Ukrainian family who had been living in St Ann's since the late 1950s. They had arrived at about the same time as the Irish and the Jamaican immigrants, and were very much part of St Ann's, engaging in all aspects of the St Ann's culture. They had made friends with the Jamaicans because of their shared understandings of immigration at the time, and their children became close friends with the black children on the estate. Consequently this Ukrainian family were considered to be 'originals' and 'St Ann's' along with the many Jamaican families, and the Irish and the white working-class families.

There were also new families and individuals moving into the neighbourhood from Jamaica, and they were more easily accepted as 'St Ann's', sometimes because they had family within the neighbourhood, but often because their culture and language, ways of dressing, and practices were already part of St Ann's, and not unusual, or hard to decode by the existing residents. There were several incidences that I came to know of where white St Ann's families had done 'favours' for black St Ann's families by marrying a relative from Jamaica in order to help them 'get their stay'. Therefore 'being St Ann's' was heavily connected to the local culture, a hybrid culture that had grown out of the estate over many years and several generations of white and black working-class families living alongside each other.

Les Back (1996), another working-class academic, noted similar findings in his research with young people in the 1990s, that within the council estate in South London where his research took place, there was a process that he called 'neighbourhood nationalism'. He noted that there were constructions of 'cultural spaces' that were extremely local, where the notion of '"race" was temporarily and superficially banished as a meaningful concept' (Back, 1996, p 51). Although this does not mean that there is a simple notion of community, where race has been ejected in favour of we are 'all the same', what is happening is that this construction of 'cultural space' is merely a space for interaction and negotiation (Back, 1996, p 51). In St Ann's there were also 'insiders' who could belong to any ethnic group, and racial boundaries had been broken down as with the Jamaicans; nevertheless, there were new boundaries being erected against the 'outsiders' who were 'culturally foreign', particularly the Iraqis, some of the Eastern Europeans and the Africans.

This means that construction of 'cultural space' in St Ann's is ongoing. There is constant negotiation of who belongs, and who is 'St Ann's'. There are specific groups in St Ann's who enter into and adhere to those negotiations, usually with each new generation passing on their knowledge and cultural resources to the next. Hence the Jamaican culture brought into St Ann's in the early 1960s is still alive, albeit taking on a different form. It has been negotiated among the residents of St Ann's, and is used as local culture and as a cultural resource by different sections of the St Ann's community. The music, food, language and dress styles of the Jamaicans have become an extremely valuable part of the fabric of St Ann's rather than belonging exclusively to the Jamaicans. It will be interesting to see over time how these new groups will negotiate and interact with St Ann's, and what happens within the estate.

While the neighbourhood offered safety from class prejudice and stigma, it also offered some safety against racial prejudice, because of the large numbers of mixed-race people and mixed families living on the estate. The neighbourhood was not only tolerant towards interracial relationships, but openly accepted and encouraged the different relationships that were made by the neighbourhood's black and white residents. All of the women who took part in this research were white and their children were mixed race, their fathers largely coming from the Jamaican St Ann's community. Racism was therefore something that most of the women talked about, particularly in relation to how 'other people' looked on their families. They knew that racism was not just something that their mixed-race children, or their partners, were subject to – many of the women had experienced different forms of racism themselves.

Some of the women had lived in other neighbourhoods in Nottingham before settling in St Ann's, and had encountered stigma and prejudice towards themselves and their families:

> **ZENA:** "I lived in Mapperley, I was the one that went out with black men, you know 'she's the one who goes out with black men'."

When Zena had lived in another area in Nottingham she described how she had 'stood out', she was different, she was 'the girl who went out with black men', but in St Ann's, she described herself and her children as 'fitting in' and as part of the community. The women with older and adult children seemed to have far more accounts of racism than those with younger children. Rona, whose eldest daughter was 19 and whose youngest daughter was six, had very different experiences with all her four children:

RONA: "Yeah, I do, I mean I remember when my eldest daughter was a baby in the pushchair and I was just coming out of a shop and a man looked into the pushchair and said 'You fucking nigger lover.'"

LISA: "Where was that?"

RONA: "In town but it was ... what 18 years ago and things were different even then to now, a lot has changed even over the last few years in town; at one point me and my girls were often stared at but we are just a normal family now ... well, especially here."

Trudy, a single mum with two daughters, also 'chose' to live in St Ann's because her daughters were mixed race. She thought that because of the amount of 'white mums' on the estate, she 'fitted in':

"I don't really go far from St Ann's, it makes you feel more comfortable here 'cos people have had years to get used to it [mixed-race relationships] so they have, and I was talking to someone the other day that there's not many families here who haven't got mixed-race kids somewhere in the family so people have had to get used to it."

The way women had been simultaneously sexualised and racialised, and subject to stigma and exclusion because of their personal relationships and their mixed-race children, was often given as a reason usually in defence for living in St Ann's. It seemed like a constant struggle for the women to explain why they lived in St Ann's in the face of such overwhelming negativity about the neighbourhood. However, all of the women said they felt valued and of value at least within the estate because of their interracial relationships and their mixed-race children. Amanda was especially proud of her daughter and her own choices. She thought that her family was doing a public service for the positives of multi-cultural Britain:

"By living here I'm doing something for the country [laughing], there has been like a boom of mixed-race children here, most

white families round here now has got a mixed-race child in
their family and that's a good thing, it breaks down barriers. I
am breaking down barriers."

Amanda valued her daughter's heritage and also found value from
her own personal choices – she was 'breaking down racial barriers'.
This view of St Ann's presented by Amanda, as a place where there
are pioneering inroads into social cohesion, is not the conclusion
you might get if you were to examine crime figures, unemployment
or health-related statistics. If you were to look at those quantitative
measurements of St Ann's, it would be easy to conclude that St
Ann's was bad for your health, career and safety. However, I have
already noted that this 'cultural space' or local space is merely a place
of interaction and negotiation (Back, 1997), which is constantly
shifting. The 'new people' on the estate are part of this negotiation,
as are the mixed families, the white working class, and the Jamaicans.
Nevertheless, the story does not end here, with St Ann's being
the absolute refuge for women who encounter stigma, prejudice
and exclusion. As I have said throughout this book, this story is a
complex account of a council estate and working-class life within
it; it acknowledges those negotiations and interactions, showing the
difficulties but also offering an insight into the more positive aspects
of council estate life.

Even though all of the women talked about racism throughout their
accounts, there were often several different ways the women thought
of racism. For some it was in the form of what they had experienced
from other white people regarding their personal relationships and
their children's heritage, although others also talked about racism
that came from black people and in particular black women. Kirsty
was the youngest woman I met. She was 19 and her baby was only
six weeks old when I met her:

"I get looks especially 'cos my boyfriend's Jamaican and he's a
lot older than me, her [baby] dad's twice my age so it was like
you get looked at for the age difference then you get looked
at the colour and obviously when I was pregnant and people
would see me with him with my big belly, it was like [gives a

look] and it was mostly from black people, from black women, you get that look of disgust."

Kirsty felt that she was subject to negative stereotypes because of her age and also because of her partner's nationality and ethnicity. Her sister Lucy, whose babyfather was also Jamaican, told me that she had encountered racism, but because Lucy and Kirsty had only ever lived in St Ann's from being small children, their experience of other communities was limited, so when I asked Lucy about racism, she told me that she had experienced it:

> "Yes, but not as much as you get it from black people, don't get me wrong, 'cos I've got just as much as a screw face and a mouth as anyone and it don't matter what colour your skin is, but there are some screw face black women look on you like you're scum and they don't agree that you're with black men; it's like they're too good to be with a white woman and some white people look on it like they're just black bastards."

I spoke to Rona, a single mum in her thirties with four daughters; she had also lived on the estate from being a child. I asked her how she thought things might be different for her own daughters:

> "I think they do have a lot more to deal with 'cos you can have a bunch of kids all the same age but all be different colours and there is still black people out there who are still racist. I think I've noticed it more with black people 'cos a lot of girls that I know who are my friends have mixed-race kids ... so if I've felt racism it is mainly with black people. I think it just boils down to that black women are jealous 'cos we've took their men away from them or they think we have, but if you sit down with black men they've got a different story to tell [laughs], it's true, yeah, but then I've got some black girls who are friends but they don't see it, that's what gets me, and there's some that don't see it and accept you for who you are or it's like 'ah yeah you've got black, well done' and they like open up their arms to you like family and then there's just others that snub you all the way down the line."

When the women I spoke to brought up the subject of how black people and especially black women had treated them, this was uncomfortable for both myself and them. Our children were not white, we all had black friends and relatives, but this came up in every conversation I had with the women in many different contexts. They knew as we talked that I must also have had similar experiences, which made it easier for them to talk about it. However, all of the women recognised that this type of racism was different, and talked about black women being unhappy about 'white women stealing their men'.

At the beginning of this section I explained that the Jamaican community had many valuable resources within the estate – and black men appeared to be the most valuable.

Jamaicanisation

All of the women I met had babyfathers who were West Indian or of West Indian descent, and the majority of the children's paternal families were Jamaican, although there were a few of the paternal families who came from other parts of the West Indies. The West Indian community and their culture have been popular with the white-working class in St Ann's, especially as the first generation of Jamaican children began to attend the local schools and built friendships with the white children. Many of the women I spoke to recounted stories of their parents in the 1960s mixing with the Jamaicans:

> **AMANDA:** "My daddy used to come into St Ann's years, years ago, and gamble with the West Indians; they used to be called the blues, shebeens, and he used to be a gambler and he used to say 'beautiful people to talk with and gamble with but I've seen how they beat their women and I don't want that for my daughter', then my mum and dad split up and he went back to Wales and my mum met up with my step-dad who is black and they are still together."

Shirley told me what St Ann's was like in the mid–1970s when she first met her babyfather:

"When we were young I used to mix in his culture and then he used to mix in mine in the working men's club so it won't just me mixing in his culture, we were in both each other's culture, we would meet up with my mam and uncles in the chase pub then we would go to the blues. I was proud of where I came from, but that din't stop me enjoying the blues as well, it was the music and the dancing and the staying out late, well, it was rebellious, the rebellious side in me, that's what it was."

Many of the women remembered 'the early days' when there were two different and separate cultures in St Ann's – the white working men's clubs, where the St Ann's English and Irish would meet, and the blues and shebeens, which were all-night illegal drinking venues run by the Jamaicans. However, most of the women's memories and experiences were of a shared St Ann's. Louise, now in her forties, with a 23-year-old daughter, recounted her experiences as a teenager:

"We went to the youth centre and met black men and black lads, I think it was 'erm ... even though I went out with some white lads, but the fun was always there with the black lads, and I think, well, you know ... how I met [daughter's] dad, it was from the King's Hall Youth Centre and I was about 17. I was walking home from my friend's house and he was washing his car and I said 'hey up' and he asked me out and that was it, if it won't for walking home I wouldn't have met him and now I wish I never did.... Bastard.... [laughing]."

However, it is the Jamaican culture and practices that have become dominant within the neighbourhood and therefore valuable, especially to the many women in St Ann's who have mixed-race children. When I spoke to Della, she told me that being part of the black British and Jamaican community in St Ann's, and engaging in the culture connected with this community, was extremely important for her, not just because she had mixed-race children:

"I've never really mixed with white people, to me to go to a white club, to me I don't feel like I fit in; if I go to a black club I

feel more comfortable because that's the kind of music I like....
I was into it even before I met the kids' dad.... I always mixed
with black people so as I say for me to go to a white club I can't
go to it 'cos I'm not into that sort of music; I feel like the people
aren't the same as me even though they're the same colour as
me ... you know people will say to me do you know you're
white. I know I'm white but it's hard to explain to someone
who don't get it."

Jamaican culture, and being identified with the Jamaican community,
was particularly important to Lorraine. She explained to me that
'black people' had always been in her life and for her, the food, music
and ways of dressing were as 'natural' as 'being Irish':

"Well, I think Irish and black mix really well, they just do, back
in the day what was it, no blacks, no dogs, no Irish, what can
you say?"

Lorraine was proud of her connection with the Jamaican community
in St Ann's and talked about her childhood memories of dancing
to reggae music, and eating West Indian food. Now that Lorraine
has her own children, she feels that it is important to cook Jamaican
food for her own family. She also told me that there was a value
attached to how 'authentic' you could make Jamaican food, and the
knowledge you had about Jamaican culture. She told me that anyone
could cook chicken, but how many women her age, white or black,
could cook good green banana:

"My auntie always went out with black guys, so I used to go
round there and she used to cook and the music was there, so
I was into it from about 10.... I like the reggae music and the
Jamaican food; I only listen to reggae music now and every day
I have to cook the food, I have to cook curries, rice, yam, green
banana, I have to cook everything; how much white woman can
cook all dem tings?"

Many of the women talked about their authenticity within the estate, and this usually meant how connected they were to the local culture which was heavily influenced by the black British and Jamaican culture. Claire left her natural mother's home when she was just 13, and moved into Shirley's home with her three children, although she told me that to start with it was 'strange' because up until that point she had not known anything about Jamaican or mixed families because her natural mother was extremely racist, and she had not been allowed to visit her school friends' homes:

> "My mum who fostered me would cook West Indian food so it was always there and some weekends, I mean, I was horrified when I first ate rice and peas, I thought God what's that, but that's because I was conditioned to mash potatoes and sausage and beans or something, and some weekends there'd be arguments 'cos Shirley would say Jamaican this weekend or English, and I would always say English but then there'd be my step-brother and sisters, Shirley's kids, who'd say, and Shirley preferably 'cos she likes spicy food, but she'd say Jamaican or English, and I'd often lose out and I used to think God if I was black would I just eat that, but then I realised that not all black people would just eat rice and peas and chicken."

However, as Claire began to fit in with Shirley's family, she started to 'feel' different – as she said to me, "not black, but not white-white either". While Claire was attending her secondary school in St Ann's, a club was set up, called the 4.30 Club. This was exclusively for black students where they could learn about 'black history and culture'. Claire wanted to go with her foster sister and brother who were mixed race, and she could not understand why she was not allowed to go:

> "I remember this club happening and all my friends signing up for it and we had an assembly about it and the headmistress explained that the club was just for black people and I remember sitting there on my chair in that assembly as she said it, getting

really angry about it, I wanted to jump up and say why … I
want to learn."

Claire was eventually allowed to attend the 4.30 Club because of
Shirley's tenacity, her unofficial foster mother, whose two mixed-race
children were attending. This is part of Claire's story, of why she is
'authentic' to St Ann's, and she said many times that she was a 'lifer'.
She could trace her St Ann's history from the severe poverty and abuse
she had experienced while living with her natural family in St Ann's,
through to living with Shirley's mixed-race family, where, as she says,
she "learned to cook food", "dance" and "plait hair", to her own life
with her daughter who is also mixed race. Claire, like many of the
women I have met in this community, enjoyed the 'authenticity' that
her knowledge of St Ann's, and the knowledge she had of the local
Jamaican culture, afforded her; she found value for herself and her
daughter within her knowledge of the neighbourhood.

Culture has become a central site in finding value, and also the rate
it is exchanged. The women on this estate, like many other women
on other council estates within the UK, experience poverty and
the absence of universal resources such as education, employment
and positive recognition. These absences and poverty mean that the
women have to maintain an appearance of order to justify their
existence; therefore culture becomes the site of exchange, in that
inclusion and exclusion, and what is intact, and consequently what
is broken, becomes cultural.

The culture, the aspirations and values of the wider population
become those of the nation, while those who do not appear to
share or achieve those cultural aspirations and values are excluded
and different because of their culture. It is right to think that in the
absence of those cultural goods that 'the rest of us' have access to,
those who do not have this access do not simply sit down and accept
their fate, but rather, they build a value system of their own which
works for them, as they have done in St Ann's, even though this only
has worth and value in their own community and sometimes similar
communities, neighbourhoods and social groups.

The local value system in St Ann's is constantly changing, however;
it is dynamic in its nature and is mediated through those who

currently live on the estate. Part of this mediation comes through their experiences of oppression and through social power relations such as class, gender and race, but also through historical understandings and processes of those relations. Part of the current value system in St Ann's relates to the mixing of the white working class and Jamaican understandings, practices and preferences. The exchange of culture between the different groups of people who live in St Ann's is central both to how people find value within this community and to the strength of the local value system.

'Black pearl precious little girl'

> Black pearl precious little girl
> Let me put you up where you belong
> Because I love you, Black pearl pretty little girl
> You been in the background much too long
> Together we'll stand so straight and so tall. (Horace Faith,
> Trojan Records, 1970)

Although the culture that is associated with the Jamaican families on the estate as I have shown so far is especially valued, it is not the only site of value – the Jamaican families themselves have value on the estate. Many of the women discussed this as being particularly significant to 'being 'St Ann's', and the value of this specific multi-cultural identity was described by the women as 'modern' and as an urban identity. Therefore it seems that mixing their own white working-class culture with an Afro-Caribbean culture created a culture and identity superior to what they described as 'the old days', when everything was 'white and boring'. The women on this estate constantly talked of the pride they had of being 'more than just white', and their 'beautiful mixed-race children', along with their modern 'multi-cultural families'. This was always discussed as the positive side of their physical, social and class positions, which they all, without exception, understood as being 'at the bottom' in Nottingham. It was this part of their lives, their own mixed identities and mixed families, that they felt was really valuable.

Many of the women discussed how they thought their children were special and beautiful, and they had given their children something of value that they did not have themselves. They had given their children a birth status 'of not being just white', which they valued, but they also knew that this was valued within the estate.

Claire's biological mother is racist, but she also recognises her mother has serious mental health issues. She remembers telling her mother that she was pregnant:

> "When she found out I was having a baby I remember her ringing and saying 'Don't ever fucking think you're bringing that dirty black bastard baby home in this house, don't ever'.... I remember taking her in the house and my mum being dead like, do I want to touch her, and I was like, be grateful, I'm bringing my daughter into this squalor.... I remember my mum holding her, but you could tell she wasn't looking at her like she looked at her other grandchildren and that, and then, me just taking my daughter back and just feeling this overwhelming feeling of protection for her, but feeling really proud of how my daughter looked, she was quite dark with thick black hair and big beautiful blue eyes, she was, and still is, beautiful."

Claire told me that her daughter also felt special, and together they enjoyed shopping at the West Indian stalls on the market for particular hair products for mixed-race people. Claire's daughter, who is nine, and has soft curly hair, asked her black friends at school to look at her hair and advise her what products she needed and where she might buy them. Claire said that her daughter felt 'very special' and 'individual' because she knew that there were hair products on sale especially for her. Claire also thought this was special for her daughter because she had to go to a particular market stall that only sold West Indian products – she told me that the West Indian people on the stall 'were helpful', and treated them as 'their own'. This may be trivial to most people, but being treated as 'special' and 'being included' within a community for Claire and her daughter was extremely important, especially considering that Claire had spent most of her life feeling worthless, and being told she was worthless by her natural mother, only feeling part of a family when she was unofficially fostered by a neighbour who happened to be white and who had mixed-race children. Being a 'good mother' to her daughter was Claire's ambition. Her ambition and hopes for her daughter were that she would be a good person, and a good neighbour, and she knew that living in St Ann's did not make you a bad person, despite what was said about it:

> "'Cos all I ever say to my daughter is all I want you to do is live
> ... live your life and enjoy it; what I don't want is for her to have
> babies at 15 ... hope she has a job and a car, I want her to love
> life and see her earning money, that's all I want in my life, to see
> her achieve and to be proud of who she is even if she is living
> in St Ann's, to be proud of that and to stick up for people and
> be proud and to be able to feel confident enough to go into
> Marks & Spencer on a one-off and treat your family to a meal.
> I want her to check on her neighbours, to be a good person."

Claire hoped that her daughter would have a better life than she had had, and she hoped that her daughter would have value as a person in her own right despite being from St Ann's. She talked of things that she valued, and hoped her daughter could achieve this value – a job, a car, being a good person by sticking up for others, and having the confidence to go into the food hall in Marks & Spencer, the things that Claire did not feel she had access to.

The women who live on this estate are very proud of their mixed-race children, and there is an 'in joke' on the estate that even though St Ann's is a poor neighbourhood in Nottingham, the kids are the best dressed – the mothers place great importance on how their children look, how well dressed they are, and also how 'good' their hair is. They spend hours plaiting and braiding and oiling their children's hair, or paying someone else on the estate to do so; any money they have they spend on the clothes their children wear, often buying expensive and designer labels.

The women I met never tired of telling me about their children. Louise, whose family was one of the Irish families within St Ann's, and who had her daughter in the early 1980s, told me that both she and her elder sister had mixed-race baby daughters and they would sing along to old Ska records:

> "We used to play records and sing 'Black pearl precious little girl', and 'Black is beautiful' to them."

Louise told me that her daughter, even though she was now 'a big woman' (adult), would always be 'a black pearl' to her, and she often looked at her and still could not believe that something so beautiful belonged to her.

Like everything here in St Ann's, the story does not stop here, with the women at least being respected and valued as mothers. They often gave their children interesting and exotic sounding names that they thought added to their children's value, such as Shanelle, Dior, Tyree and Ymani. However, as in almost everything that the women on this estate did, the names of their children had two values – the value inside the estate and among those who understood and worked within this particular value system, and the value outside of the estate, among those who did not understand this value system. These types of names are associated as 'Black names and are deemed as low status' (Edwards and Caballero, 2008, p 41). On the estate the names are thought of as special and exotic, but among those who do not share this particular value system, they are ridiculed, stigmatised and devalued. In 2005 the BBC reported on findings related to children's names in an article on their website, 'Children's names "spell trouble"', that teachers were making snap judgements about children from their names. It was reported that teachers were particularly wary of children who had exotic or 'chav'-sounding names such as Charmaine or Jordan, while names like Charlotte and Joseph usually meant 'delightful children'. This example of how the children's names were valued on the estate but often became sites of ridicule on the outside helps us to understand how culture can become the site of how value is negotiated. 'Good taste' is that which belongs to the middle class, it is normal and respectable (Skeggs, 1997). By glamorising their children's names the women's 'taste' for the exotic is ridiculed, becoming signifiers of bad taste, common and 'chav-like'. Their use of the exotic, their mixed-race children, and exotic-sounding names, which they believe moved them away from the valueless positions of being poor and working class, are again subject to misrecognition, disrespect and add another marker to how they are known by 'the rest of us' outside the estate.

Once you go black you never go back

This valued understanding of 'blackness' and Jamaican culture on the estate is heavily associated with black West Indian masculinity linked with street and urban culture, incorporating language, music, food and dress. This is a specific understanding of masculinity and is recognised as extremely prestigious in and around the estate. Even though this local understanding is linked to black urban masculinity, you do not necessarily have to be 'black' or male in order to benefit from its value. Academics studying in the field of culture, such as Dick Hebidge (1979, 1983), Roger Hewitt (1986), Stuart Hall (1990), Les Back (1996) and Paul Gilroy (2000), have, over the last 30 years, mapped how heavily stereotyped images of black masculinity, particularly the fantasies regarding sexual potency, black men being 'uber cool', through music, style and ways of speaking as well as their link to criminality, and macho aggression, have infiltrated the British psyche, especially within white working-class youth culture.

St Ann's in Nottingham has all the elements that allow the creative processes of 'black culture to be re-made' in negotiation with the white-working class residents. This is an extremely interesting and important use of people sharing space and culture that has emerged in St Ann's, and allows another dimension in understanding contemporary classed identities. Sharing culture, in heavily classed spaces such as urban council estates, can explain new ways in how value, class and belongng can be understood. And it is not only the white mothers on this estate who have mixed-race children who engage in this hybrid and entwined culture of 'blackness', and 'working classness' – it is widely understood and practised throughout the estate. Claire explained to me what she saw within the estate and how this particular understanding of 'blackness' in practice worked:

"You see these white guys trying to walk like black people and you think God it must take you all day to get across the street but you're prepared to do it, to keep this image, and they have this tough face and you think 'you're not black'."

This is only one of many observations by the women in this research of how 'blackness' was often practised within the estate, especially by young white men who appeared to practise 'being authentic' within the community through the visual markers of ways of dressing, walking and speaking. In fact, many of the women struggled to explain their own 'feelings' of ethnicity. Gina, a 21-year-old single mum of two boys, told me:

"I don't see myself as full white, neither do my friends, especially black friends. I don't think they see me as white or a white person, they know I'm white but they look at you different, you know, 'cos you've got mixed-race kids."

Gina extended this complexity to her personal relationships:

"Yeah, I have tried to go out with a white boy before but the white boys think they're black, they've got gold teeth, they've got the black image, so you might as well go out with someone real."

When Gina talks about 'someone real' she is talking about 'authenticity' on the estate, and what is real and authentic for Gina is the black male, who also holds the most value for her. She demonstrates this in this next extract in how she thinks about 'white men':

"It might seem horrible but you know, I think boring old white pub man, and I think of my dad who just plays football and I know black people play football, you know, but I just think like beer belly and how they dress, and then black people, it is different, you know, you can go to all these different dances, different music, food and it's interesting."

Both the men and women in St Ann's understand the value and worth of 'black culture' and how it is used and appropriated within the neighbourhood.

Kirsty and Lucy were two sisters I met who had been born in Glasgow and came to St Ann's as very young children. They told me that although they were essentially Scottish, they felt very much part of St Ann's, and also part of the 'black community'. Their family had moved into a council house on the estate when Kirsty was only three years old and Lucy was a baby in the mid-1980s. Both had Jamaican babyfathers and both used Jamaican patois within their everyday language:

> Lucy: "People has said to me 'you think you're black 'cos you talk like that', well actually, no, I don't, I see it as street even now I'd get it as a big woman [adult] in the pub, you know, people say, why you speak like that, and I'm, well, that's how I've always spoke."

Kirsty, who was 19, and had a six-week old baby daughter when I first met her, also spoke in a strong Jamaican patois, and like Lucy, defended this way of speaking:

> "Well, a lot of people have said that I think I'm black and I wanna be black but I don't see it like that, I see it like it was the community I was brought up in, you know, if you stick a black person in a white community they're gonna grow up white and if you stick a white person in a black community they're obviously gonna have black ways about them."

The sisters saw themselves as 'authentic' in St Ann's. They had grown up on the estate, and had engaged in the local culture, they both had black friends and both were in relationships with Jamaican black men. They were well known on the estate and therefore 'fitted in'; they had adopted an identity that they described as 'street'. The St Ann's identity that is valued within the estate is both local and national as it draws on the ongoing class-centred disadvantages within the UK. It is also international as it incorporates the practices of different migrant workers, in this case, Jamaicans, who have settled and shared their culture. They were often accused as 'wanting to be black', which they both rejected, but they also rejected a white identity, opting for 'Scottie Yardie' as a way of explaining their families. They both recognised the importance of the identity that had been passed on to them through their immediate Scottish family, but they also wanted recognition for the culture they felt they have been brought up with from the streets of their community, which they recognised as Jamaican. They discussed how their family photo would now look in relation to when they were children, as both their partners were black, and their children were mixed race, and used this analogy to explain that they were no longer a 'white' family. This was common throughout the estate. While all of the women acknowledged themselves as 'white', many tried to explain, often in great depth, why and how they were 'different' to other white people. Many showed me photographs of their family weddings, christenings and other get togethers.

Within the estate I noted many times how the word 'white' was being used as a disparaging term, usually through 'piss taking'. On one occasion I was in the community centre. It was 'rice 'n peas 'n chicken' day, and there were a few of us sat eating; there were also lots of kids as it was half-term. One of the women who was sitting with us got up to go over to the fish and chip shop. She had decided not to have the Jamaican food that was on sale that day in the community centre. As she got up, one of the women asked her where she was going, and when she said she was going to the chip shop, another woman started laughing and called her 'white'. Although all of the women were white, the word 'white' was used to 'take the piss' out of her choice of English over Jamaican food. I have also heard 'English' used in the community in a similar and disparaging way, in particular when relating to clothing. The young people on the estate often use the words 'white' or 'English' when 'cussing' someone's clothing, particularly training shoes – 'white man's trainers', or 'English man's trainers' are usually the ultimate 'cuss'. Appropriating this local culture, and engaging in the local value system through what you wear, eat and how you speak, is a matter of embodied social practice, a constant reiteration and 'performance' of particular discourses. The particular discourse here is of people who have become known as 'socially excluded' outside of the norms of society. Their understandings of who they are have both been informed inside the estate where they feel comfortable and fit in, but also by how they are judged and viewed, often harshly, outside of their community. Recognising who you are is a constant negotiation through dialogue, partly overt, partly internal, with others.

It is through these practices, and this dialogue of recognition on the estate, which determines how 'authentic' you are. All of the women I spoke to recognised these practices and engaged in them despite age – although this type of street culture is often associated with young people and youth, in St Ann's it is associated with 'being local' and 'being St Ann's'. Dawn had three children – the eldest two were white, and her youngest was mixed race. She told me that:

> "Well you have to fit, you have to fit like … I've been here all my life, it's funny really 'cos when I go out, 'cos most of my friends are either black or mixed race. I think I've probably only got three or four white people who are my friends … and, for instance, I was out a couple of months ago with a white friend and we went to a pub where she likes to go and it was a white pub and I felt uncomfortable."

Dawn went on to say where she did feel comfortable, which she described as 'black places':

> "I feel like I fit in that kind of place, I feel like I slip in a lot better. I love the music, that's my music … I play the music for all three of my kids and my daughter, she's white and she understands patois and sings to all the words."

This connection to what they call 'black culture' and the 'black community' was important to the women – they felt like people of value on the estate through this engagement. But it was often more than this. They also felt they might be valued outside of estate through the concept of multi-culturalism, but not through being white and working class. When the women spoke of the things they did like about St Ann's, multi-culturalism was something they often brought up. The next excerpt is part of a conversation between Tanya and her mum Sharon while they were discussing all the things they liked about St Ann's. The primary schools were again well regarded, and as many women have told me, they believed their children were getting something really important by going to school in St Ann's – 'multi-culturalism' was often brought up as the extra value that their children were gaining. All-white neighbourhoods and schools were never appealing to the women on this estate. Sharon thought that she was also gaining something from the neighbourhoods' ethnic mix; as she said, "it's us, the lower class ones" who are mixing, and she believed that could only be a good thing:

> TANYA: "That's one of the positive things about St Ann's for the fact is that if you go to certain areas where the kids are all white, then them kids have a thing there like a barrier with them people ... 'cos they haven't mixed with them when they've mixed and they're all multi-cultural and they have had to learn things and then even in the classrooms here in St Ann's, the teachers teach them what comes from the Chinese people and whatever else there is round here and that's good, our kids don't grow up ignorant, they know about multi-cultural things and that's good."

> SHARON: "I think that Sycamore is a good school, they do loads of things for multi-cultural things ... yeah, they need to know about all different cultures, the white and the black culture, that's what I think is important, both."

> TANYA: "I believe that there should be more multi-cultural teaching 'cos it's alright having them all together and them not learning from each other, I think it should be a topic at all schools like Art, Maths and English, yes, because this is a multi-cultural country now."

> SHARON: "Well, I think that eventually this country will be mixed race 'cos there's that many black and white people going together, there's a lot of mixed race 'cos it's not the richer ones that are mixing, it's us the lower ones, so maybe our class will not

be white anymore, we will end up mixed race, well, that means
that life's more interesting for us 'cos life was boring when I
was young. I've found out that it's more interesting being with
a black man, put it this way, I've done more since I've been with
them and I've learnt more and seen more than when I was with
a white man."

Although it has often been argued that multi-culturalism is a vague
and confused concept, having different meanings to different people,
the people in St Ann's explained their relationships, families and
community as multi-cultural, and understood it as a sharing of
culture, 'mixing it up'. The women often used the Jamaican national
statement, 'out of many comes one people', as a way of explaining
what St Ann's has within its boundaries, and how it should be viewed.
One community, many differences, but ultimately 'being St Ann's' is
important and is by having this shared understanding. Sharon, who
was in her fifties and had eight children, six of whom were white, had
a specific understanding of multi-culturalism and what it meant to
her on a personal level. She told me that her life was more 'interesting'
now, and being with her black partner had given her value within
the estate that she had not experienced previously:

"You used to go to parties and there was boring food, but now
it's all different food, different music, yeah, I am proud of my
mixed relationship."

As Sharon explained, she, like all of the women on the estate, was
extremely proud of her mixed-race family, and the thought of the
white working class no longer being white was not a worrying
prospect for her; in actual fact, many of the women on the estate
thought that having 'mixed families are good for us'.

These positives should not be underestimated. Although there were
problems on the estate with other migrant groups such as the Iraqis
and the Africans, these tensions were usually spoken of regarding
housing, problems getting doctors appointments, and queuing in the
Post Office, in addition to the amount of single Middle Eastern men
living on the estate. The tensions were never spoken of regarding

the women's children mixing with other children from different backgrounds – 'mixing' was always seen as positive within the local schools. 'Mixing' in St Ann's is a process of integration, but it is a two-way process. In this case respect is an important point as it was the lack of respect, and recognition as a group, which the poor white working-class have often been denied. Respect and positive recognition is an especially important issue for the white women in this book, and they have managed to find positive recognition, at least within the estate, through their association with 'black men' and 'black culture'.

This association with black men is a complex issue – although the women found respect on the estate through their personal relationships, they knew this was often not the case outside the estate. And it was often difficult for them to talk about their personal relationships with black men because of the way they were sexualised through this association. It seems that 'falling in love' and being with your life partner who happened to be black was one thing, but admitting to being attracted exclusively to black men was something else, and it was difficult for the women to talk about. It took many meetings and a great deal of trust; however, eventually, almost all of the women I spoke to said they could not see themselves being with a white man in the future. Kirsty and Lucy told me that they could not really see themselves with white men even though their mum had asked them why Jamaicans in particular:

KIRSTY: "My mum was telling me just till yesterday to get rid of him [boyfriend] and find yourself a nice man, not so much a nice likkle white bouy."

LUCY: "A decent English black man will do."

KIRSTY: "It's gone to the stage now that we are never gonna settle down in the near future with a white man."

LUCY: "So you might as well get a decent English man even if he is black, that's what she says."

KIRSTY: "If it's gonna be a black one get an English one, I think she's racist."

LUCY: "She isn't."

I often asked the women I met, whether it was because they had mixed-race children that they would not consider going out with a white man. As Alison told me, it was down to her preference:

> "I do … actually find black men well very appealing, very appealing, well, I think all that was, because, well, the different culture and well … an unknown fascination to you … you know, like an attraction that you can't see, I don't know, I am one of those women who are just attracted to black men, there is a lot of women here in St Ann's like that."

Alison, now in her forties, had been around black people her whole life, and recognised that there had been significant changes, especially over the last 10 years, in how you were perceived within St Ann's when you were a white mother to a mixed-race child. She knew that there had been an increase in respect when you were associated with 'black people'. This was very different from when she had been young, when you were more likely to have been disrespected. She told me that as she was growing up in St Ann's and began to hang around the black guys on the estate, there was a saying that the black guys used to say to the white girls in the 1970s and 1980s – 'once you go black you never go back' – and she thought this was true for her at least, and now said it in a light-hearted way to the younger women she came across.

Rice 'n peas 'n chicken

Even though it is difficult to show and to write about the complexities of the racial framework in St Ann's, when there are clear antagonisms between newly arriving migrants from Africa and the Middle East, at the same time the women clearly valued and engaged in many aspects of Jamaican cultural resources, while consistently speaking of prejudices they had experienced, predominantly from black women. There is a real complexity here, and I am not denying the existence of racism towards white people by black people, especially when many of the women described what they had experienced as racism. There was an understanding that there was competition among the women for the limited resources available to them. I have argued throughout the book that within this estate there are limited social resources such as housing, healthcare, good education for the children, and decent prospects for employment. There was also an acknowledgement that some of the resentments that black women might have for white women who had black partners were forms of competition for cultural and symbolic resources – and in this particular context the resources were not only black men, but also the Jamaican culture.

> **AMANDA:** "Well, I know the young girls now, they wear the big gold earrings and the black hair styles and I think that's all to do with competition."

Amanda talked about the competition she had both seen and experienced over the years for black men, but she also explained how this competition had manifested itself through local practices, style and fashion. She told me in the 1970s and 1980s that the black women in the neighbourhood really made an effort in having 'white hairstyles' in order to compete with the white woman's 'good hair', but explained that now in St Ann's it was the white girls who were adapting their style and fashion to compete again for black men, by adopting black styles of dressing.

The two friends I met who spent most of their time together, Sonia and Shelley, were talking about their mixed relationships. Sonia was always defensive whenever we talked about 'mixed relationships'; she was never comfortable about talking, or even acknowledging, mixed relationships, and always asked me why I was so interested in white women exclusively, whether I brought up the subject or any of the other women as we chatted. Sonia often avoided talking about being in a mixed relationship, but as her friend was talking one day about a young girl she knew who had just had a baby, the question came up about why so many white girls had mixed-race babies:

> **SHELLEY:** "Have you heard [girl's name] has had her baby, he's called Dior."

> **SONIA:** "Is it Jermaine's baby?"

> **SHELLEY:** "[laughing] Another one of your breed [speaking to her son]."

> **LISA:** "There's a lot of mixed-race babies now here, more than even when my son was little. Why do you think that is?"

> **SONIA:** "'Cos of white women [laughing], what do you have to ask that for?"

> **LISA:** "It's a fair question."

> **SONIA:** "Why, what are you saying, that black people are more attractive? What can you say to that question?"

As we sat and ate in the community centre, a few of us were talking about the music being played. It was Damien Marley's 'Welcome to Jamrock'. We were discussing that Damian Marley was the most talented out of the Marley family, and his mother had been a white woman who was also Miss Jamaica. We began talking again about mixed relationships, and this time Sonia engaged more fully in the conversation:

> "Well, you do sometimes get them feelings that you shouldn't say it, are them black people gonna look at me a certain way 'cos I'm white and should I listen to the music, you do feel angst about that, that you shouldn't be listening to it 'cos you're white, but so what, well it's like the other week my husband was at his sister's and this this black lady walked in while he was having somert [something] to eat, rice 'n peas 'n chicken and she said

to him, I bet you wish your wife could do food like that, don't yer, well he made her look so small, he said, listen, yer see when my wife does her rice and peas her rice comes out red, and she said, well, I have to give it to her 'cos I'm black and I can't get it red, you see, she tried to out me down as a white woman even though I won't [wasn't] there."

Sonia talked about the 'angst' she often felt when she engaged in what she called 'black culture'. She feared that she might be judged for being white and not having a legitimate entitlement to listen to the music, or to cook the food. The neighbourhood hierarchies here in St Ann's are difficult to understand, but the women spoken about them. Sonia knew that being a white woman was another 'less than'. The dominant culture in St Ann's has been heavily influenced by Jamaican culture, and for many of the white working class in the neighbourhood, reggae music, Jamaican food and 'black styles' of dressing have become the visible markers that 'being St Ann's' embodies. These markers have become extremely valuable within the local value system. While at Shirley's house one afternoon we were arguing with her 18-year-old daughter Rachel, who is mixed race, and Rachel's friend, who is white, about the size of their earrings:

SHIRLEY: "Some of her friends won't go out with white boys 'cos they tell me it's unfashionable."

RACHEL: "But saying that there, there are some mixed-race girls and black girls who go out with white boys who wanna be black."

SHIRLEY: "It's like [daughter's friend] I say to her, tek them earnings out, you look ridiculous, even yardie girls [Jamaican girls] don't wear earrings that big, you can wear 'em as bracelets, duck, put 'em on your wrists not in your ears ... and I'm straightforward, I'm against white people wanting to be black, but I've got a pride in myself and of my colour, yer see, I was always proud of myself, I used to fight with black girls all the time ... they still give me dirty looks, they thought I should be

at the bottom and they should be above me, but I didn't think
that, you see, here in St Ann's it's all switched round, black men
at the top with black women then mixed race that we created
then us, white women and white men, at the bottom."

Shirley explained the 'pecking order' in St Ann's as she saw it: black
men at the top, then black women, mixed race, which, as she stated
"we created", and then white women followed by white men. This
was often discussed by the women on the estate, not always as clear
as Shirley explained it, but there was a general acknowledgement
that the women in this community placed a much higher value on
all things Jamaican.

The women in St Ann's found value and worth from what was
available locally; these resources helped make their lives a little
easier, and they had a use-value to them that had no transferable
value outside the estate. They made up the local value system and
were recognised as valuable by those who engaged in that system.
There was nothing wrong or subversive in wearing big gold-hooped
earrings or expensive Gucci sunglasses when you lived in a council
house on benefits; rather, it acquired meaning and significance only
in its relation to its context, when transferable sources of value were
not available. What we must never forget is what these cultural
signifiers mean to those who employ them, and also how they are
interpreted by those who do not and who are watching from the
outside. So wearing large gold earrings, having gold teeth or wearing
branded sportswear shows the deep entrenchment of how arbitrary
social hierarchies on the body are interpreted. This is an important
argument because when individuals and groups, and especially those
from poor neighbourhoods and low social class positions, engage in
social practices, social networks, cultural practices and ideas that are
not recognised and therefore misunderstood by the wider population,
these practices are either invisible, or of no value, or count against
them.

Respect, recognition and status

Respect and status within the estate was constantly spoken about – 'giving respect' and 'being respected' was always something that both the men and women on the estate were aware of, so being respected became central in most stories. As discussed earlier, the women on the estate were angry and hurt by the way they often felt 'disrespected' and 'misrecognised' as people with no value, although respect on the estate was found through the valuing of local identities and local practices. I spoke to Lucy, whose babyfather was Jamaican and who had invested heavily into a form of black, and in particular, Jamaican, culture. Lucy told me that when you were brought up in St Ann's you had to act in a certain way otherwise you would be disrespected and bullied:

> "Well, I was rude when I was ready, I was rude, I don't care who you are, if you're not my mum or my dad I don't business [care], if you look at me in a certain way I'm gonna cuss yer, I can make you feel small with my mouth alone … that's just me, I had to grow like that, I had to be kind of wickeder [worse] if you like, than the rest of them to prove a point, you know, that you can't take the piss out of me because I'm white, regardless of being white, I'm still a person and so are you in the same way … as I don't like look at you as you're ignorant 'cos you're black, don't look at me as sarff [soft] because I'm white 'cos I'm wickeder than you and you."

Lucy was explaining that within the estate there were certain codes and understandings – if you were white, and in particular a white girl, you had something to prove, you had to prove that you were not 'soft', otherwise there was a chance you would be disrespected and bullied. Lucy told me how the process of 'being respected' worked in practice, but also the implications for young white women, and men:

> **LUCY:** 'Really, yeah, in St Ann's there is a status and they play on it, I think with a lot of white girls there's a status of going out with a black guy, they put them on a pedestal and they forget

that their dads are white and that their dads are a good man and their dads brought them up and he wasn't black, they think that to be with a black man is the be all and end all."

LISA: "Why do you think that is?"

LUCY: 'I don't know, I don't know.... It's just the way it is ... there is a big thing to be with a black man, I think it's because they think they're wicked and they like that bad boy image."

LISA: "Do you think it's that bad boy image?"

LUCY: "Yeah, I think it is, but then again, some of them white buoys [boys] are just as bad if not worse 'cos they're trying to have that image and trying to have that persona like them ... they're not gonna progress in life, they're just gonna end up in prison or out on the streets although I can understand why they're out on the streets 'cos the money's there ... bin there done that, but the money's there, why go and slave for somebody for a pittance when you know you're not gonna get any thing for it."

Lucy understood the 'street respect', the status that can be given within the estate, but she understood the downside of this, having to constantly think about being 'wickeder' than anyone else, the image that must be maintained, and ultimately, how this might end up in a person going to prison. It was not just about being with a black man, it was what 'being with a black man' represented: street credibility, a reputation and respect and a status within the estate.

The start position for the women on this estate, as they saw it, was social rejection. Therefore in order to be a person of value, and a valued person, the women used the local value system that was available to them, which also made sense to them: it worked. The wider and universal system (Bourdieu, 1986, p 52), where education can be exchanged in the open market for economic capital, prestige and status, does not apply within poor council estates, and is rarely proven as worth investing in. So the people who live on council estates invest in what does work for them, through what is available, and worth investing in. Education, training and even employment do not always 'pay off' within council estates; while wages are being driven down in real terms, and higher education is a risk, and often feared, the universal system that Bourdieu terms 'the symbolic economy' moves further away from the poorest people.

Therefore the practices that offer status and respect within this social group become extremely important, and were often spoken about in many different ways and contexts. How you dress, how you look, what food and music you prefer, and in this particular case in Nottingham, being connected to valuable resources such as 'black masculinity' becomes an opportunity to obtain prestige and status, at least within the estate. As stated earlier, you do not have to be black or male in order to benefit from this resource – the women on this estate benefited by association from their personal relationships and also through their mixed-race children.

The interests, beliefs, practices and other people that matter most to the women on this estate were not simply things that they happened to like or prefer, but things in terms of which their identities were formed and also to which they were committed, even when those interests, beliefs and practices were pursued and could have a negative effect on the individual. The women on the estate invested in particular practices in order to 'fit in', and to 'be St Ann's'. They valued the local resources that were available to them and engaged in those local practices in order to feel valued and worthy – they were available to them, they were accessible and proven.

What the women engaged in within the estate and valued, for example, 'fitting in', 'being known', engaging in what they referred to as 'black culture' in the way they looked, spoke and cooked, were not simply resources 'for and on the inside'; these preferences, practices and values also created an inside, they were simultaneously 'St Ann's' while creating what it meant to be St Ann's. Therefore, having established that 'being St Ann's' was valuable and valued within the neighbourhood, allowing the women and their children to 'be known' offered some safety within the estate, and gave access to a social life. In order to 'be St Ann's' there are cultural markers that say that 'you belong', and that you are 'authentic', and therefore it seems that local inclusion to those who are socially excluded becomes ever important.

5

'On road, don't watch that'

There are many sayings and phrases that are used on the estate, and they make perfect sense. The people who live on this estate, and probably in estates all over the UK, have an uncanny knack of saying something that is so succinct, getting to the heart of what is needed, in ways I have never known in other areas of my life. In the academic world the practice is, I believe, why say something in 100 words when you can say it 10,000? In working-class communities the opposite is true – one phrase can explain a whole essay of practice. One of my favourite phrases is a relatively new phrase and that is, 'don't watch that'. This means exactly what it says – 'don't watch', 'don't look', but more importantly, 'don't see' and 'don't be interested'. I have heard this used in many ways. One of the men in the gym was on his phone talking to a woman who was not his girlfriend; when the other men asked him who he was speaking to, his response was, 'don't watch that'. I have heard other men say it when they are 'doing business' on the street and neighbours might be having a look, and I have heard women say it to each other, especially when discussing their taste in clothing, and if you ask where they bought something or how much something cost. I have also seen arguments and fights break out over 'watching' when someone has commented on another's action/behaviour/practice. The common response is, 'why you watching me?' – 'don't watch that'. Having this type of 'insider' knowledge, but understanding why it is important, has meant that I have become close to many of the residents in this community, and I have been allowed to see and know many parts of people's lives that would be difficult to understand without this insider knowledge. I am trusted because I don't judge, I accept how things are, and I understand that in 'getting by', hard choices and decisions are often made within families. And as long as I respect this code, my 'watching' is tolerated.

Local inclusion and social exclusion

After reading this far about this neighbourhood, many will be asking, why would anyone want to stay and live on this estate? The milkman was beaten up, there is drug dealing, and if you live on the estate 'others' – those outside the estate – know you as a person of little value; 'rough and ready', you struggle to get a pizza delivered, and your children see the world through metal gates. However, the men and women who live on this estate *want* to stay; they feel safe.

I have explained how important safety is to the men and women who live in St Ann's, but also the protection of their profile. This is why watching and judging and commenting is not tolerated, it is protection of your profile. When you are devalued to such an extent and you are known as a person with little taste with no resources to the outside of the estate protection of profile and your person can become defensive.

Consequently, the residents construed safety in many ways – the processes and the way safety is understood is multidimensional and complex. Personal safety, feeling safe walking around the estate, safety from class prejudice and racism were noted as important. And there was a need to be safe from stigma, their fear of 'being looked down on' because of misunderstandings, misrecognition and disrespect for their lifestyles by those who did not live on the estate. Therefore belonging to the estate, and 'being St Ann's', were ways that the residents on this estate mapped out geographical space, and also emotional boundaries, as defensive means.

While boundaries were put up by those who lived on the estate in order to feel safe, or, as Loic Wacquant says (2008, p 47), 'as a screen to shield against the prejudice of the external', at the same time those boundaries acted as a wall, keeping in a closed and suspicious group of people, whose fear of stigma and 'being looked down on' often prevented them from engaging in pursuits that might make real and positive differences to their lives. Throughout this book I have described a tight-knit community, which has been built on pride, a sense of belonging, humour, and sharing, but also fear, instability and stigmatisation.

Lynsey Hanley, in her book *Estates* (2007), calls this 'estatism', how the council estate where you live seeps into your soul, you belong to it, and it belongs to you – these feelings are often unconscious, but more commonly feelings of belonging are spoken of regularly, and actively sought by the residents. This is how 'estatism' works; it is a reciprocal dynamic of fear, prejudice and resentment, protecting those who engage in it to some extent, but also causing immense amounts of damage.

The defensive measures of 'keeping safe' undoubtedly took a heavy toll on the everyday practices of many of the families involved in this research. Lorraine often spoke about safety in many different contexts because the last 10 years of her life had been especially chaotic. Even though she described herself as 'streetwise' and able to cope with the problems in St Ann's, she admitted that sometimes she felt 'frightened' by what was happening 'on the street':

"Well I would say that the alleys and rat runs round here, I'd say it's not too good like with violence. I always hear people screaming and sometimes I go out, it's all related to drugs."

I asked her whether she went outside when she heard screaming:

"Well, you know, what I do and I've only just learnt that now is keep away from it 'cos you could get hurt and that was only till a couple of months ago and that was 'cos I went out and there was this guy battering a woman and it was over drugs, right, and he sort of got nasty to me until I walked away, right ... and I would normally go out and try and think that I'd probably know the person 'cos they're from round here and say like 'come on it's not worth it' but it was like, it was two people and I did know the lady but I din't [didn't] know the man, and he got quite nasty with me, so now I've learnt that I'm gonna have to blank it unless I knew that one of my kids won't [wasn't] in, then I would definitely be running out."

Feelings of 'belonging' and local inclusion were evoked in complex ways – as Lorraine said, she assumed that she would know anyone who was in the St Ann's area, that she would be safe even in dangerous situations because she would be recognised. For Lorraine, the danger comes when there are people on the estate she doesn't know or who don't know her.

However, Tanya and Alan understood belonging to the neighbourhood in the ways they were involved in the neighbourhood, and also how well known they were. Both volunteered in the community centre. Alan had taken a course at a local college and was now qualified as a chef. Neither Alan nor Tanya had ever 'officially' worked, but in order to get some experience of running a business and a cafe they volunteered at the community centre and cooked for the locals at lunchtime. It was a Tuesday and very busy because the small market was on in the precinct, and it was 'curry goat and rice 'n peas day', the most popular dish in the centre. As we talked about the unofficial local events that often took place in St Ann's, particularly through the summer, Tanya told me that Alan had a

'sound crew' (mobile reggae/ragga/dancehall disco). He was also the
volunteer van driver for the community non-profit launderette in
St Ann's. As a consequence Tanya and Alan were very 'well known'
and a popular couple within St Ann's. Alan often set up the 'sound'
in his front garden and people would come round.

> Tanya: "I do things in the community 'cos him [Alan] does a lot
> for the community and I do things around him to put events on
> to try and get the kids off the street and that's all voluntary that
> I do … in summer we have dances all over the estate, everyone
> comes and brings a lickle [little] drink and some chicken, we all
> have a good time and get together till late."

Tanya and Alan's 'events' were widely spoken of within the estate,
and many people on the estate enjoyed these impromptu events
throughout the summer. They could take their kids and meet up with
other people from the neighbourhood, but only if you were known
to the family or within the neighbourhood. Tanya told me that she
had at 'least one hundred' people on the estate she would call family,
and Alan had about the same – even though many of these people
might not be blood relatives, they were people they had grown up
with, or they had intermarried within their families. I have attended
many of the events held in Alan's front garden, as well as the events
he has held in other parts of St Ann's. They are usually centred on
family events, children's birthdays, christenings, and even weddings.
Dancehall and reggae music is played really loudly, everyone brings
a drink, and the mutton, chicken and rice that Alan cooks is paid for
by whoever's party it is, or, on the day, by everyone who eats 'putting
in'. There are usually the same people there, including many of the
women and their children who have taken part in this research, but
apart from Alan's brothers, cousins and sons, not so many men. Most
of the young people in the immediate area turn up; no one seems
to mind as long as they behave, and when they don't, there is always
someone there to tell them to 'fuck off'. Most of the street is out
and taking part in the event, or sitting in their gardens listening to
the music, so no one seems to complain, and the police have never
been called. Loud music coming out of people's homes is a feature

of St Ann's in the summer, and has been cited by many as one of the things they like about the neighbourhood.

The complexity of 'belonging' could be fragile in one discussion, or more grounded and robust in another, especially when 'belonging' meant being safe. Amanda, who had worked as a street prostitute for many years and who understood the dangers of being in certain parts of St Ann's, especially at night, used her sense of being locally included as a measurement of safety, and local inclusion was a resource you needed if you wanted to live in St Ann's safely. She specifically related this to stereotypes and fear around black men:

> "Yes, I believe it is a safe place to bring your children into, it's safe 'cos we are all classed as working-class black and white, we all have some things in common, the children feel comfortable in places like this with each other you know…. I've been pissed up at 4 o'clock in the morning and I've seen a gang of yute [youth] hanging about and they've gone 'white Manda y'alright' and I've just gone 'yeah I'm alright' and they've gone 'you wan me fe walk you ome' and I've gone 'no leave me man' with the keys in my hand, but if I was somewhere like Bestwood Park or Arnold, I wouldn't be able to do that, I think it's because we know the area, it's our territory you see, when you have lived round black people a long time you get to know how they are, like, if you see a group of young black guys in town and they're just having a laugh with each other, you see people looking frightened and moving out their way when all I see is a group of kids laughing … that's people's ignorance, they've been conditioned because they don't know how black people are, it's like when you see kids with their hoods up, I see kids, other people might see danger."

Being included in the local neighbourhood, and therefore the feelings of belonging, were central in promoting and feeling a sense of safety. Amanda felt safe in the neighbourhood even at night because she was known, but also because of the knowledge she had about the culture of the neighbourhood. Therefore, as Amanda explained, it was not only important to 'be known', but also to have a specific knowledge that could only be gained from being part of the community, and locally included. However, local inclusion meant more than just 'being known' on the estate. When Amanda talked to the 'yute' at 4 o'clock in the morning, she spoke in Jamaican patois, showing that she was not only known, but she had a cultural connection to the estate and to the youths. Like many of the men and women on the estate, Amanda had adopted a hybrid way of speaking. This was one of those cultural markers of local practice, local inclusion, one of many connected to the Jamaican community, which said clearly you were 'St Ann's'.

In addition to 'feeling safe' and having respite from 'being looked down on', being 'part of St Ann's' had other benefits. It also allowed a social life, being included in official and unofficial social events. Although there were events and family parties in the local pubs, the last remaining pub closed down at the end of 2013, and I am not sure what impact that will have on the estate.

Council estates as places of safety

The general rhetoric regarding council estates, and in particular the people who live on them, has emphasised the importance of geographical location, and estates like St Ann's are as Polly Toynbee noted in 1998, 'perceived to be ghettoes of the workless and the hopeless' (p 22), areas that *The Sunday Times* described as 'morally, spiritually and emotionally disconnected from the rest of society' (Phillips, 1998). In response to Karen Mathews' arrest for kidnapping her own child, the media found blame in a defunct culture breeding within Britain's council estates and their residents. As Carole Malone wrote for *News of the World*:

> "People who'd never had jobs, never wanted one, people who expected the state to fund every illegitimate child they had – not to mention their drink, drug and smoking habits…. A whole legion of people who contribute nothing to society yet believe it owes them a living – good-for-nothing scroungers who have no morals, no compassion, no sense of responsibility and who are incapable of feeling love or guilt. (Malone, 2008, p 15)

While politicians report, and media coverage paints, a bleakly homogeneous landscape of social alienation and abandonment of hope, the people who live on this estate in Nottingham tell of a far more complexly textured life – they speak of adaptation, cooperation and a reflexive awareness of their lives. Their accounts are inflected with recognition of heterogeneity and a sense of positive as well as negative aspects of estate life.

The men and women who took part in this research regarded St Ann's as a place of safety, which may seem a contradiction, bearing in mind the problems the estate has with crime, especially crime and anti-social behaviour resulting from the local drug economy. However, those who live in this community invested in the neighbourhood in many ways, spent much of their time in St Ann's, and thought of themselves as 'St Ann's'. As the men and women increasingly engaged with the estate, it seemed they stood out more from what their perception was of 'normal Nottingham', outside the estate. Zena told me that she rarely left the estate unless she was 'going into town shopping':

> "I think it's safe if you live here because people know who you are, it's not safe if you don't live here and you're walking through at night, so yeah, you are better off living here if you come here.... I never used to go out a lot 'cos I had all this paranoia that people were out to get me, you know, but since I've moved down here, I've started going out ... from living here, yeah, it's quite easy to make loads of friends, 'erm this stereotype that St Ann's has got it's not like that at all, 'erm ... it would be, if you're not from here it probably would be."

Dawn, another single mum with three children, has lived in St Ann's for most of her life. She said that she had 'no problems in St Ann's' and had no plans for leaving, but she was aware that her position of 'being well known' gave her an advantage of how freely she could travel through the estate as opposed to those who lived on the estate and were not well known:

"Some people are scared to go out now ... some people who
live here don't know anybody who lives here now and they've
tried to sell their houses but they can't 'cos it's in St Ann's ...
but there again, I don't have no problems here in St Ann's, I get
on with a lot of people and I am very well known and so are
my kids, we go wherever we want in St Ann's, the dealers on the
'chase' [shopping precinct] just say 'y'alright'."

St Ann's is extremely important to the families who live here in
many ways, particularly in how their association with St Ann's affects
how they view themselves, both positively and negatively. Apart
from 'town' (the city centre), most residents told me they had little
or no contact with other areas within Nottingham or even wider,
and their social life was firmly located within the neighbourhood.
Having family, friends and a close social network within the estate
was important to the men and women, and therefore what happened
and how you could operate within St Ann's was essential in living
there. Consequently, it was extremely important that you 'fitted in',
and 'being known' was particularly important.

This was important to the women, and to the mothers who were
constantly aware of their own and their children's safety, particularly
when they talked about the practicalities of their daily lives as mothers.
Most of the women used informal childcare, other women picking
up their children from school, and babysitting in the evenings or
at weekends; this allowed many of the women to have a social life.
There was also importance around safety and your children 'being
known' as they played out on the streets – the women told me that
often other women, neighbours or friends or other children had
brought back their own children after they had been hurt while
playing. Describing why she felt safe in St Ann's, Mandy described a
recurring situation with her 16-year-old son who has severe learning
difficulties and is autistic:

"Well he [son] you have to watch him like a hawk because the
minute you turn your back he's off.... I have had to phone the
police to look for him so many times 'cos he struggles with the
roads and he could easily be killed but everyone knows us round

here and when he's escaped, usually someone has seen him or even the kids bring him back."

Mandy was also aware that outside the estate, where she was not known, that her son could often draw unwanted and negative attention, which was often difficult for her, and therefore staying within the boundaries of the estate was especially important to her and to her children:

> "I couldn't really go to any places with him because of how he behaved and I was always scared with what people would say about him and what they thought of me and how they judge you, 'oh look at her with that naughty boy' you know."

For Mandy, 'being known' was important for her son's safety; because she had lived in St Ann's 'all her life' her son was less likely to get bullied because of his learning difficulties as he was known as 'Mandy's lad' or 'Remy's' brother (Mandy's eldest son). Mandy's son had always attended local schools with specialist tuition, so Mandy thought that it gave all the kids on the estate a chance to "get used to him and know him".

Mandy went on to tell me that she had once lived outside of St Ann's when she had fallen into rent arrears with the council, and because she was 'not known' in the new neighbourhood, she could not let her children out to play because they were also not known. Consequently she very rarely left the house so as not to have 'to explain' anything about her children; she became very depressed and ill at this point in her life until a social worker helped her to return to St Ann's. Therefore for Mandy, and for many of the women on the estate, 'being known' and 'fitting in' meant the difference between having some quality of life, and no quality.

Staying in St Ann's for many of the women seemed the 'safest' and often the only option. Lorraine told me that she would "probably always stay in St Ann's" – she knew a lot of people, and had some local support. She had recently started volunteering at the prostitute outreach service that had been set up by women who had been involved in prostitution from St Ann's:

"I want better things now, that's what I mean, you know, I've started to get involved with things 'cos before I've sat back, but I do want to help people and myself now ... but I always say to my kids and say to people, do you know if I ever won the lottery or anything like that I'd buy this house and have it the way I wanted, probably take my driving lessons and get myself a car but still be me and do whatever I could to help people here, and people say, no, you wun't, you'd go out and you'd buy this posh house and I say no, I wun't, I'd have this house how I wanted and stay right here where I am, there's nothing wrong with the area, it's the people, and we can change if we want to."

However, Lorraine knew that not everyone on the estate could be safe within it – St Ann's only offered partial safety and then only if you were 'St Ann's', so 'becoming St Ann's' was both a resource and a necessity. 'Being St Ann's' and living in St Ann's are not the same things, however; the women could positively identify themselves through 'being St Ann's', even though being a resident of a council estate through mainstream understandings is not a valued identity. 'Being St Ann's' meant safety in St Ann's. Lorraine recognised this and knew that other council estates offered similar safety for those who 'belonged to it'; she knew that this type of safety could not be offered to her in other neighbourhoods, because she and her children were 'St Ann's'. When I asked her whether she would leave the neighbourhood, she told me:

"No, no, I don't know why 'cos this place's a shit hole [laughing], I don't know 'cos it is such a shit hole, and I think it's 'cos of being so young and growing here, I mean, and then, like, I wouldn't say that I get problems as in problems 'cos there is a lot of people who move round here who don't know nobody, right, that do get problems, and when I see that it makes me think that God, if I went into another area ... with my kids as well with the way they are I'm definitely gonna have problems, do you know what I mean."

'Being safe' was often used as a key reason why many of the women chose to live or to stay in St Ann's; this might seem controversial because of what is thought to be known about the estate. Therefore being part of St Ann's and being widely known was valued highly by the women in this community – it allowed freedom to move within the estate, which many of the respondents understood was not available to all.

Safety from class prejudice

The feelings of safety that the women often articulated through their sense of 'belonging' to the estate appeared to be as much about feeling excluded from what they called 'normal society' or 'out there' as it was about belonging to St Ann's. In the last chapter the women clearly said that they knew 'others looked down on them', and that services such as the housing office and benefit agencies made them 'feel excluded' and 'not good enough'. When I spoke to the women about the way 'others looked down on them', I asked whether they thought this was related to social class. Very few of the women talked about social class, and even when I asked them, they were not sure if they were working class because as many said, "I'm not working". However, they often said where they thought they were positioned; as one woman answered, "pretty much at the bottom of the pile" or "lower class". Most of the women understood this in several ways – some thought this was because of where they lived, others because they were benefit claimants, and those who were lone mothers usually thought that their single-parent status 'classed them'. Sharon, who was in her fifties, was one of the few women who had a good understanding of what it meant to be 'working class' in the traditional sense because her father had been a trade union shop steward as a builder. Her daughter Tanya, who was 27, also understood the concept of class through her grandparents:

> TANYA: "I know what that means, my granddad and grandma were working class and they went out to work, like my dad worked all his life and mum, she even worked and done all jobs like worked in cleaning places, cob shops still, when we were

growing up, we never had free school meals when we were at school, never, none of that, we have always had our parents work for us."

LISA: "Do you still call yourself working class now?"

SHARON: "I just call myself a housewife and I'm like, well, on social so I'm like a housewife who looks after the children, I've got two grandkids here and my own two children so I would just say I look after the children."

However, Sharon told me she used to be working class, and she knew this because of her father, but also because she had worked in the local factories in Nottingham until the early 1980s. She did not think of herself in this way now, because as she said, she was not in paid work and was 'on the social', despite being the only carer for her own two children, her two grandchildren and her 80-year-old mother. Sharon's daughter, Tanya, also understood that being working class was about being proud of working, not relying on the state, and not having free school meals – both their understandings 'of being working class' left them unsure of where they fitted in society now.

Moving out, and staying in Stannzville

Understanding your place in the world, where you belong, and in particular, where you are not welcome, are issues that the people here in St Ann's know very well. The lack of social justice and class disadvantage also includes a debate about 'space' for those who cannot or do not want to 'move' up or out.

Mobility was a big issue for the men and women on the estate; they told me time and again that they had to put up with things from which others can could move. They discussed this with me in many ways – their feelings of being 'trapped' in stigma, which was often exacerbated when they said they did not want to 'move out' because St Ann's was their home, that they were often thought of as 'unreasonable', as Lorraine's social worker suggested, or had no sense of aspiration, or were simply 'deficient'. This type of 'fixity', in other words, where residents find it difficult to move and have little power to move out, helps distinguish the poorest working class from 'others', and when we can easily recognise them, they become easier to move away from. The locatedness of the poorest people in the UK is a class distinction, in particular, the naming of council estates as shorthand meaning 'rough', 'bad' or 'immoral', and the sense of criminality, danger and filth that names of council estates conjure up in the imagination. These namings, as I have argued throughout, have two meanings – what they mean to those who do not live with this stigma, and also they hold meanings for those who do, affecting how they see themselves, and also how they understand their relationship to the neighbourhood. It then becomes apparent that the idea of mobility becomes ever important within any discourse relating to inequality and social justice.

This particularly relates to young people and the mothers on the estate who very rarely went outside the physical and emotional boundaries of St Ann's (an emotional boundary is the space that is imagined to belong to one group or another, and is only adhered to by those groups – the term 'estatism' may be useful here). This is not straightforward, and is a highly complex issue, with complex rules of engagement. There are parts of the commercial city centre in Nottingham that have imagined boundaries within certain groups and are known by those groups to belong to one group or another. Victoria Centre shopping mall, Footlocker sports shop and the McDonald's situated near to Victoria Centre shopping mall are all places that are known within certain groups of young people to belong to St Ann's. This is in relation to other parts of the city centre that belong to the Meadows estate, Broadmarsh shopping mall and the McDonald's close to that centre. In addition there are other areas in Nottingham such as the Forest Recreation Ground, where the annual Goose Fair is held, that belongs to the Raddyman (Radford, another neighbourhood in Nottingham city centre). This is until the annual Caribbean Carnival is held, and then there are spaces and boundaries within it – different music tents then become bounded by whoever has the greatest representation on the day. These boundaries go largely unseen and unknown within Nottingham, but there are sometimes incidents that bring them to life, and make them observable to some people at some points.

Lorraine understood the boundaries and 'fixity' in a particular way because of her association with the gangs in the neighbourhood:

"We shun't [shouldn't] all be sticking to one part, it's like going to Broadmarsh, we know we're safe in Vic centre, but it's like, what Meadows think about Vic centre, 'I don't want to go up in Vic centre 'cos of Stannz man', we used to walk through all them shopping centres and feel quite relaxed but not now."

There are many incidents within Nottingham regarding mobility, and the emotional and imagined boundaries become extremely important. During 2008 in the Victoria Centre shopping mall in Nottingham, a group of young men from Radford, a rival neighbourhood to St Ann's, were shopping in one of the sports shops in the St Ann's side of the centre; they had dared to enter too far into Stannz territory and as they were Raddyman it was seen as being blatantly disrespectful. Within 10 minutes there were 15 hooded and scarved young men from St Ann's in the sports shop with guns, knives and baseball bats. There was a stand-off because the Raddyman also had guns. No one was arrested, although some of the Raddyman were injured; those with guns and weapons left before the police turned up. Surprisingly this was not reported in any of the local or national media, even though a large part of the shopping centre had to be closed off. These incidents are not uncommon within the city; however, they are rarely reported on.

These boundaries of who can go, and who belongs where, also extend to the service providers within Nottingham. They are all too keen to provide services within the estate. Many of the women whose children were over 16 attended college courses at the local youth clubs and community centres, usually basic numeracy and literacy classes, IT and NVQs in business skills; these courses are provided by local colleges who send in tutors to teach within the estate. There are also mentoring programmes that over-18s can get involved with. This involves mentoring younger children within the estate at youth clubs and community centres. These schemes are considered helpful to the community as it is assumed that people within the estate cannot be motivated to leave. The BBC's 'Inside Out' programme featured the mentoring programme within St Ann's in January 2005, which it hailed as a 'progressive method':

> The headlines say it all – another murder, another gun crime, another murder victim. Nottingham's inner city has become synonymous with violence, gun crime and communities in crisis. People in St Ann's have had enough of the tragic waste of human life and living in constant fear. (BBC 'Inside Out', 21 January 2005)

After speaking to some of the mentors, the programme claimed that:

> As a result a 'mentor' feels more valued in his own community, "I've got respect from where I am and from around my way." (BBC 'Inside Out', 21 January 2005)

This is a very simplistic approach to exclusion and disadvantage, which accepts rather than challenges people's often-limited horizons and poverty of opportunity, and works within a limited framework. Being respected in your community is not the problem; it is being respected outside the neighbourhood that residents of council estates struggle with. And it seems that mobility within this council estate, whether social or actual, is becoming more and more difficult daily. For the 'mentors' and students from St Ann's who spend all of their time in that locality, after a time it becomes very difficult to move out through fear of stigmatisation – they know they are limited, in that they do not have the education or the skills or the money or the value, and so opt to work and stay within the community, not feeling comfortable outside. I am not suggesting that people who live on council estates should be motivated to leave and live somewhere else, but what I am arguing here is that through fear of not knowing how you may be treated and viewed by unknown others, unhealthy emotional attachments are made to a neighbourhood, particularly by the young, making it more difficult to make positive networks outside of the estate but also within it. Because the people in the neighbourhood rarely make those external connections and networks, their ideas and skills remain stunted. Therefore the potential skills, knowledge and talent within a poor neighbourhood very rarely become realised, when they could be used to influence positive change within the neighbourhood.

The fear and uncertainty of leaving your neighbourhood has unintended consequences for those who have been positioned as 'lacking'; they do not simply accept it, however, but find value and worth through other routes, often through local neighbourhood inclusion. 'Estatism' is the negative side to that value; it is what happens when groups who live on council estates stop engaging with the outside, through fear or stigma, or ridicule, and become only inward-looking. This has particularly devastating outcomes when there is a relentless and dynamic underground economy, usually linked to drug dealing, and also because of the ever-tightening grip that 'estatism' has over those who live in the neighbourhood; the problems that families on the estate endure, and their reactions to them are also dynamic in their adjustments.

I have discussed in parts of this book the problems this neighbourhood has had with the drug economy, and also its association with gang culture and estatism. These three parts of this overall problem are all interlinked, and in different ways. Although the drug economy as it is today on the estate is a fairly recent problem, it stems back to the mid-1990s. Over this period St Ann's has become the main drug dealing neighbourhood in Nottingham, with a large majority of Nottingham's registered drug users. There are also many more transient groups coming in and out of the neighbourhood to 'score' (buy drugs). This has led to an increase in drug dealing on the estate, particularly the practice called 'shotting'. 'Shotters' are usually the low-level drug dealers carrying and holding low levels of heroin and crack cocaine, a couple of hundred pounds' worth; they are usually quite young, sometimes as young as 13 and 14, and are predominantly black, mixed race and male. They are given a 'spot' by the older dealers, one or two rungs up on the ladder, and can earn about £50-150 a day. They often employ even younger children as 'spotters' and 'watchers' who look out for the police, or rival dealers, and these children can be as young as six or seven. These

163

'shotters' carry the most risk of being arrested as they are the most visible, and are 'holding' (carrying drugs) around the estate. They are organised by slightly older local men who have worked their way up the ladder. These men have more respect, and money, and drive around the estate in their cars, or hire taxis to carry them around the estate. So ensuring that St Ann's is the main neighbourhood in Nottingham for drug dealing is a priority for them – this is their 'endz' (land, neighbourhood, patch), sometimes referred to as Stannz, SV or Stannzville, and the business of drug dealing is very lucrative. The defending of the 'endz' has therefore become a key aim for the lower echelons of the drug economy. Within St Ann's there are several semi-organised groups of young men who have 'spots'; some are heavily associated with the drug economy, while others are only loosely connected, or have no connection at all. The largest and best known gangs in St Ann's were the Cadburys, Brewsters and Bad Breed. The Cadburys and Brewsters are neighbourhoods within St Ann's and represent drug-dealing spots. However, they have now joined up and become one large gang representing the drug-dealing spots in St Ann's, and are now called Street Life. The third gang, Bad Breed, was a gang that was exclusively mixed-race young people, and their 'bad breed' identity was important to them; however, they have recently opened to any St Ann's youth, and are no longer exclusively mixed race. They are a relatively new gang on the estate but are very quickly becoming notorious for the level of 'badness' they are engaging in, from robberies to street attacks. The term 'bad breed' is an old Jamaican term meaning mixed race – the elderly Jamaicans on estate might refer to mixed-race people as 'bad breeds', 'half-breeds' and 'cut breeds', or sometimes just 'breeds'.

There was low-level animosity between the different gangs in St Ann's, but since they have joined into two larger gangs, Street Life and Bad Breed, the real competition is now between other neighbourhoods in Nottingham – the Meadows and Radford – which are also drug-dealing neighbourhoods. On a street level, whoever you are in St Ann's, by living there you are considered as Stannz or Stannzman, and the same goes for Meadows and Radford. This is what 'estatism' means, a form of territorialism, which is not always linked to the drug economy as it encompasses a much wider group of residents. Children as young as three and four can understand and engage in estatism – through their allegiance to Stannz, they sing songs and raps about other neighbourhoods that have been made up by older children in order to 'cuss' other estates.

There is a non-profit-making clothes shop on the 'Chase' (the local precinct) which sells t-shirts, beads and other clothing that represents the neighbourhood, made and designed by the young people at the local Youth Inclusion Project. The t-shirts sometimes commemorate young people who have died on the estate, with the words RIP to whomever they are commemorating; often there is SV, or NG3, printed on them; and the beads they sell are the colours of the estate – in the case of St Ann's, they are red. Estatism here in St Ann's is about 'being St Ann's', belonging and connection, and the loyalty you have to your estate.

Over the years the level of understanding on the estate at what is happening within the gang and drug culture has become well known. I have not come across a single person as yet who resides in St Ann's, either young or old, or from any background, who does not have knowledge of the extent to which that these practices are affecting the neighbourhood. The women on the estate are acutely aware of the drug and gang culture on the estate, either because they are directly involved with it, usually through sons, partners or other male family members, or indirectly, because of the problems it brings to the estate. The amount of drug users and prostitutes attracted to the estate because of the drug economy, and the problems that arise when crack houses are in full swing, or as the park becomes unsafe, are issues the mothers have brought up and have been represented within this book. In Chapter 2 I discussed the drug users and the contempt some of the women had regarding the 'cats' and 'fiends' coming into the neighbourhood. This often caused tension on the estate:

"And then there's the mums who say they don't know what their kids are doing, yes, they do know what their fucking kids are doing, where did they get their £200 trainers from? And they say 'I can't do anything', yes they can."

One of the women I spoke to told me that she knew that her son was involved with gangs and drug dealing and she had reported him to the police because of the effect he was having on his younger siblings:

> "It's more difficult for me to control my kids, yeah, and when you've got one child who's doing the gun thing then the others are looking to that one … but the police don't do fuck all."

Some of the women I spoke with were aware of what their teenage sons were involved with, and although they had fears around their sons' engagement in the drug and gang culture in St Ann's, in some ways they were complicit with it:

> "I try not to beat myself up about it anymore, I'm proud that my son breathes today, that's it, the way he is he does things which aren't legal but he makes money and he's still alive, for now."

I got to know this woman quite well and met her several times in the community centre for coffee; on this particular day, however, she was upset and agitated. When I asked her if there was anything wrong, she told me:

> "I got a phone call from one of my son's friends this morning asking me if my son was dead, it had gone round on MSN that my son had been killed last night and everybody in St Ann's knew that this was true, so I had to get hold of him this morning to find out whether it was true. I have to get hold of him every night or I speak to him every night and that's stupid 'cos what's that about, then every night I know that he's in danger with others 'cos of what he's involved in and you know what, I mean I got that phone call this morning and he'd not stayed at home last night so my mind was ticking over into allsorts … yeah, I had to get hold of him this morning and say to him that your name's gone round MSN and you were meant to have been killed last night and he knew something about it so something had happened, what he didn't say, but that's the worrying aspect of it, do you know what I mean, he knows something, now I've

got to go out to see if he's involved in something again and when does it stop, when does it stop, it stops when they're either dead or locked up, one or the other, I mean they never grow out of it 'cos they always think they're missing something, if they're not down here, they're all took in by it Tupac wannabes, they'll end up dead or they'll end up in penn [jail] for a long time."

This woman was speaking about her 16-year-old son, who she knew was involved in low-level drug dealing and heavily involved in the gang culture within St Ann's. Although she told me that she was afraid that he might be killed on the streets, or that he might 'go to jail', she had some respect for her son's independence; as she told me, "he's making money", and he was respected within the estate, and he was respectful of her, which ultimately meant that as his mother, she was also respected on the estate by the other young people involved in similar practices:

"Yeah, but at the end of the day, he [son] always comes through to me and how he represents outside, he's not bringing through to me ... I know he's dealing with guns and I know what's going off in his life and that's all I'm bothered about, if he's dissing [disrespecting] me then there's no point, is there, 'cos if he can diss me or disrespect me and I'm just nothing then, and he can just walk all over me."

Another woman told me that sometimes, when she went into the community centre, some of the younger girls who were involved with YIP would try and intimidate her:

"She come out with some nasty comment and that intimidates me and makes me feel like I don't want to go to that community centre but there again, as soon as they find out who my son is, they're all over me, you see, he's [son] a bit of a big boy down there."

Because her son was respected 'on the street' and had a reputation within the St Ann's gangs, it meant that when any of the young people who would hang around the community centre knew who her son was, she was 'respected' and made to feel welcome within the community centre. She told me that his reputation had benefits for her, as she enjoyed spending time in the community centre with the young people who went there.

I have said from the start of this book that the story here in St Ann's is complex – the lives of the men and women here are both simultaneously positive in the way they feel about their children, how they have pride in their neighbourhood, and their efforts to live in a place where many would find impossible, but there are also negative aspects – some of the women tacitly encourage their children's involvement in criminal behaviour, and they do so because they believe that the local value system in St Ann's is the best way, or the only way, that they or their children can be valued, and their choice in partner is often made within that same value system – they choose men who are valued and respected on the estate, as this brings with it value and respect for them.

6

'The roof is on fire': despair, fear and civil unrest

Throughout this book I have discussed the many problems facing the people who live in this neighbourhood, how precarious their lives are, and also how resilient they have become, using their community networks to find value for themselves, their families and their neighbourhood. However, I have also noted the consequences for communities, families and individuals who live with such constant instability. What happens to such communities when they live on the tightrope, when any wobble can knock them off, unbalance them or frighten them? Changes in Housing Benefit can render them homeless. Work and employment can move from neighbourhoods with little notice – in the space of only a few years whole sectors of industry can close and move on to another region or country. And decisions made for you and about you can mean new people move into your neighbourhood who are also vulnerable, who you do not know, and who do not understand. Consequently, and because of this constant state of precariousness, community networks become close; as people rely on each other and the neighbourhood for some stability, they become very inward-looking, and fear what is outside of the neighbourhood.

These people experience institutionalised stigmatisation and the instability of constantly changing social policy that always seems to be aimed at them, leaving them with little confidence that they are valuable or valued in wider society. Accordingly, this level of instability, lack of confidence and fear can lead to negative practices – people become angry and sometimes aggressive. The frustration of everyday life here in St Ann's can be seen and witnessed on the streets and in the community centre, where there may be arguments and fights between residents. In the doctors surgery and the housing office, in local shops and at local schools, you can often hear the desperate frustration that manifests itself into shouting and raised voices, sometimes between queuing residents, and sometimes with those who work in these places. Although poor communities can be both a place of safety and a place where you can be valued, as I have shown in earlier chapters, they can also be a pressure cooker, filled with fear, anger, desperation and fragility. And a dangerous mix of inequality and lack of social justice kept in small spaces, without routes in or out, may sometimes explode.

Badness and 'fuckery', fear and hostility

One of the criticisms that has been levelled at research looking at poor working-class neighbourhoods, and in particular council estates, is that they are often sanitised, or with a clear heroic narrative of victims overcoming adversity. Those who research and write about working-class life may not want to engage with the fear and anger, hostility and violence that can be part of such precarious lives. For many researchers and authors it might be the case that they do not want to risk further stigmatising the research neighbourhood, as I have wrestled with throughout this book. This is especially true of those researchers who come from working-class backgrounds. And sometimes those who research poor neighbourhoods and who are not from working-class backgrounds may not witness or recognise the extreme anger and frustration that is such a part of working-class lives. Often those who live in poor neighbourhoods know what to say when they are asked about their lives from middle-class researchers, journalists and professionals coming into the area. They know they must be the 'deserving poor' – they are acutely aware of the differences between the 'deserving' and the 'undeserving', the 'shirker' versus 'striver' narrative. They know these differences are clear-cut and uncomplicated for those who do not live with such disadvantages.

The men and women in St Ann's often spoke of how those within wider Nottingham judged this neighbourhood, but they also knew that they were often judged for other aspects of their lives – their single-parent status, welfare dependency, being white mothers to mixed-race children, the neighbourhood connection to criminality, and the stereotyped image of the black man from St Ann's selling drugs. They often said that they felt 'that everything was always against them', and there was a general hostility always aimed at them, particularly whenever they read newspaper articles about council estates, single mothers or television programmes that were about 'benefit scroungers', and whenever politicians talked about a new policy that involved 'getting people off' benefits. The men and women I met took this personally – they said that it felt like they were under attack, and they were extremely angry about how they felt both misrepresented and misunderstood.

The two sisters I met, Della and Julie, were without doubt two of the angriest women I have probably ever met. When I first met them in Della's home, it was an uncomfortable and difficult experience because of the anger and overwhelming despair of their situation. I wrote in my research diary afterwards:

> Julie was really angry for the whole three-and-a-half hours I
> spent with her today, I felt that she was angry at me, at least she

aimed her anger at me, her sister just kept saying "Why is it so hard, why is it so hard?" I didn't know what to say, I just feel depressed. (taken from research diary, 1 March 2007)

When I arrived at Della's house her front window was boarded up, and although I arrived at 11 in the morning, there were already several young men hanging around outside her home. Della told me they were 'shotters' (young drug runners), and outside her house was 'their spot'. When I entered her living room it was dark because of the boarded window, and the only light was the light coming from the television. Both Della and Julie are single parents, and both claim Income Support and Housing Benefit, as did many of the women on the estate. They were both acutely aware of the condemnation that wider society has of women in their situation.

Julie was particularly angry about how the government had, as she said, "abandoned certain people":

> "I think the government just let us live in a bad situation knowing we'll deal with it and live with it how we need to ... who are they to condemn our lives? They wouldn't even live with us, they wouldn't even live a day in our lives ... do you know what, I've got enough just taking on my one, making sure that he's [son] safe without having to kick the government up the backside to mek [make] them do what should be done, anyway, as long as I can look after my one I can't be bothered about anyone else, I have to look after me myself and mine and that's it."

Julie told me that life was 'hard enough' for her and she found it difficult to think about making long-term plans – she had to live day by day and see what happened, which she said made her frustrated and angry at almost everything. Della was also angry and frustrated, but she explained that she often felt powerless and unable to do anything about it:

> "There's no incentive, they want all these one-parent families to come off benefits but they don't make it easy to do it, they don't know the circumstances that you're in ... it might be alright for

one person to go to work but for another it's not, it's not feasible for me to go to work, I'd be killing myself to get to work, getting someone to look after the kids, I will have to be up till midnight trying to cook meals for everyone – who will make sure that my house runs properly when I am at work? I'd end up killing myself for what, £10 or £20 extra a week ... I worked until I had my second to last child, I worked from when I left school. I had a Saturday job and they took me on when I left school but I've always had a job, even three jobs cleaning and working behind bars, just crap jobs basically, but I worked and I was proud of the fact that I still worked, but I was in a relationship where he was a lazy wanker, he wouldn't get up and do anything, so I had to rely on my kids to look after each other when I was at work, he weren't in or he was in bed, so I had to make sure that all the meals were cooked before and after I went to work and I only had three kids then ... so for me to go to work now it would kill me, it is hard, it is hard to make something of yourself when you've had kids at a young age ... and I didn't ... if I had known I wouldn't have made the mistakes ... you would listen to your parents, you would know that they were bringing you up properly and you wouldn't fail in life, but life, it isn't that simple, is it?"

As Della talked about the problems she encountered, she was extremely angry about her situation, not just because of the difficulties she might have trying to work with five children as a single mum, but because she knew very well that by working she would lose her state benefits and be only marginally better off, and it seemed to her that no one else could see this. Her frustration was also with herself – as she said, "I wouldn't listen". She also considered herself a "failure in life", and this was not an unusual response from the women. Lorraine, who had recently been released from prison, acknowledged that her situation was, as she said, "dire"; she was really struggling in the house she lived in. She explained that the council had given her the house she had previously lived in before she spent time in prison; this had been difficult for her and her children as she had been arrested and remanded straight to prison from the house in front of her children, and they had been taken by social workers into care. All of Lorraine's belongings, she later found out, had been put in a skip outside, and as she explained to me, on her release from prison, she noticed that some of her neighbours had her furniture and carpets in their homes.

I asked Lorraine whether she was angry about the way the council had treated her, and she said that she "couldn't be bothered thinking about it anymore". The housing department and social services wanted to help her to secure a tenancy and to get the children out of foster care, but they explained that 'limited resources' had given them no option but to offer her this particular house as she did not want to move to a different estate. Her social worker 'felt she was being unreasonable'. Nevertheless, Lorraine described herself as someone who "wouldn't listen", and blamed herself for the problems she had encountered; she told me that as a young person she had been more interested in "getting into 'badness and fuckery'".

When we talked about education, she told me that by the age of 15, like most of the women on the estate, she had had enough:

> "I din't get a good education but I went a different way in life and left when I was 15 … and no, but that was only my own fault, that wasn't the school not educating me, I was in foster care and kept running away."

Lorraine had been placed in foster care herself after her own mother left and went back to Ireland, but she felt that the problems in her life were of her own making – as she said, she should have listened to the adults around her "rather than keep running away".

Other women I spoke also took full responsibility for the problems that they were now experiencing; they described this as "not trying" or "it's my fault" or "I didn't care" – many of these statements came about from reflecting on their school days or when they were younger, before they had children.

Ella was in her mid-forties when I met her, and she had three grown-up daughters; she also cared for her brother who had severe learning difficulties. Ella felt that she was in another difficult period of her life, one that she felt very frightened about. She had had her children when she was a teenager, and apart from cleaning jobs, she had not worked for a long time, was frightened of the future and did not know what would happen to her. Ella's brother was about to go and live in a secure nursing unit, and as she said to me, she was "really frightened" because she had never really learned how to read and write properly:

> "I suppose they [teachers] weren't really bothered about me, but there again, I don't know how much attention I put in, and I think in my third year I started bunking off, so I suppose in the last two years of my school, I weren't really there, and on one of my reports they said I wasn't there so they couldn't say anything … I had to take my brother to school, I must have had to have some kind of explanation why I had to be late every day, but all I got on my report was hmm … was lateness, lateness, lateness, so hmm … so probably 'cos my friends were bunking off I followed suit, I just followed, probably on the last year of school, I probably went there a few times and that was it."

When Ella left school it was 1979, and despite hardly being able to read and write, she went to work in a factory but did not "really get on with it" – she said she kept catching herself in the machinery. After that she went to work at Woolworths, and then she had her first daughter when she was 18, followed by two more within a few years. Even though she had been through many 'tough times', living in homeless hostels with her children, struggling with money when they were young, she said that she was really afraid now because she knew she had to go back to work:

> "Well, I suppose I'll go back to work but my job will have to be a basic job, won't it, just to earn money, it won't be a good wage but hopefully enough … I'm not sure if I will be alright, I'll have to be, won't I? It does bother me because I won't be able to help the kids out, I'd like to help them out if I can, but as long as I've got [partner's name] I'll be fine, he will help me out … if I could stick education I would go back, but I don't think I will be able."

Ella was not unusual as many of the women I spoke to thought that their lives were now "pretty much set in stone". Therefore for many of the women in this study the irredeemable 'mistakes' had been made as children or as young adults, and they took responsibility for them into their adult lives. These are the same people who are often accused of not taking responsibility for themselves and for their children.

Fear mixed with anger and self-blame were common responses from the women in this community when they discussed their lives; they often had regrets about their education, wishing, as Ella had told me, "that someone had said something" about her not attending school. However, as adult women and mothers, they often felt overwhelmed by their circumstances, and frustrated that life, for them, seemed so difficult.

During this period of the research, I found myself reflecting on my own life. I have similar experiences to the women, I, too, have been homeless and afraid, done too much too young, and I am not exempt from the fear and anger that often consumes residents on council estates. At this point I found it extremely difficult to go into university – my own anger and feelings of helplessness were often made worse by the optimism and opportunities and excitement for the future that many of the students at the university epitomised.

These feelings of fear and anger that are ever-present within this council estate are often complex and were difficult feelings for the women to try and unravel. There was often acute fear around competition for the limited resources on the estate, whether they were social or physical resources such as housing and state benefits, or symbolic resources such as value and respect. This could be difficult for the women to articulate – they told me that competition within the neighbourhood for resources such as healthcare, social security benefits and social housing had given rise to hostility between different groups on the estate, particularly newly arrived migrants.

The women in St Ann's were acutely aware of how accusations were played with of 'white working-class racism' when communities complained about pressure on local services when migrants have been moved into a neighbourhood. This was particularly difficult for the women in this community to articulate, a result of their awareness and understandings of migration and racism because of their mixed-race

children and their interracial relationships. St Ann's has a long history
with migration, and migration is still a feature of St Ann's today, as
there are new migrants moving into the neighbourhood from Eastern
Europe, Africa and the Middle East. When I spoke to Julie and Della,
they discussed their frustrations about the added pressure on the
neighbourhood which they felt was coming from migrants moving
in to the community; they saw this as a policy decision coming from
above, and something else they had no control over, "another part of
the avalanche". They also believed that St Ann's was particularly and
unfairly under pressure, as migrants were never moved into more
affluent areas within Nottingham. This did not mean, however, that
they had no sympathies with those they described as 'asylum seekers':

JULIE: 'We've got all the asylum seekers in St Ann's, look how
many problems we've had in St Ann's, now we've got to integrate
with them as well … they have put all them asylum seekers here
and I haven't got nothing against none of them, believe me, give
them a roof if they need one, but why can't they have one in
Ruddington as well as putting them in here with us, we've got
our own way of living and now we have to try and adapt to
them or them to us … how's that work, then, 'cos where they
come from, they come from a more fuckery place than this, I
understand what they have probably gone through, but it's just
more pressure."

DELLA: "I look at it different still … they just the same as us,
they've been flinged here among all this lot, imagine how they
feel, 'we've left where we was and now we've come to this', St
Ann's, where they see people getting shot, they thought they was
coming out of it, how do you win?"

JULIE: "I know, some of them have come from good jobs in
their own countries and come here for what – to what – they're
not really gonna get accepted, you know, they're gonna get the
most amount of shit … and nothing ever changes for us, so do
you know what, I'll just go with the flow of it now, I'll talk to you
all day 'cos nothing's really gonna change, is it, we all know this."

DELLA: "We have to make the best of it."

JULIE: "Make the best of a bad situation."

The dominant narrative here, relating to being poor and living on a council estate, is yet again about feeling powerless, having no say, and being disrespected. The women who live in St Ann's argue that their community is being used as a 'dumping ground', 'a scrap yard for people', and a place where 'they' put people who 'they' do not know what to do with. Both Della and Julie questioned whether the problems they saw within their community were being replicated within other areas of the city, especially those areas that they understood as wealthy.

These feelings of insecurity about territory, status and power, where material rewards are unevenly distributed and are continually shifting, leaves people with the feeling that they are constantly on insecure ground, which encourages boundary erection. These insecure feelings often manifested themselves through anger and distrust of anyone the women felt might profit from the difficult situations that they encountered. This sometimes meant that there was real hostility between groups within the neighbourhoods, but there was also hostility towards those neighbourhoods that the women believed were kept free of problems at the expense of St Ann's.

Lorraine was particularly unhappy because she thought that St Ann's had been targeted by the council to put the 'foreigners':

"When I was a kid you seen blacks, whites and probably the odd Paki [Pakistani], and now you're seeing Kosovans, Polish, Africans, every nationalities that you think of, I think this is where they stick 'em 'cos it's such a shit hole, they're mixing us up and causing all sorts of problems [laughing] ... nobody should be discriminated against 'cos of the colour of their skin, I don't think, but when it comes to foreigners and things like that and sticking 'em all in with us, blocking 'em in all one area and I'm thingy about it ... well I'm not being nasty or nothing, but I mean, I see Iraqis and I see how they look at the kids, do you know what I mean, watching 'em, following 'em down the

road … they have asked me for business nuff [many] times on
my way to the Co-op and I've got a thing about that, you know
what I mean."

As Lorraine said, she was unhappy that every day, on her way to the
local supermarket in the precinct, she was asked, by a group of men
she referred to as 'Iraqis', 'for business', meaning, was she selling sex?
Lorraine was not sure whether these men thought she was a prostitute,
or whether they were asking all women for business; nevertheless,
she felt angry and disrespected by these incidences. Other women
I spoke to in the neighbourhood were having similar experiences.
One woman told me that she and a group of women had joined
together and 'battered' (physically attacked) "one of the Iraqi asylum
seekers" for asking to buy sex from one of the women's 15-year-
old daughters. When I spoke to this woman about the incident, she
said, "Why should we be the only ones having to put up with this?"
The women understood this as 'the council' disrespecting their
neighbourhood by putting people into it without thinking about the
impact it might have, but they also had an awareness that there were
other neighbourhoods in Nottingham that did not have this level of
incoming new migrants. Although they vented their anger about the
'new people' coming and living on the estate, they were very careful
to say that it was not because they were foreign, and it was not racism
– for them, it was about being disrespected, their neighbourhood
being disrespected, and the fear and insecurity brought about by the
inequalities they were witnessing within Nottingham.

These hurt and angry feelings that the women had within the
neighbourhood were not only vented towards 'asylum seekers' or
migrants. They told me that it was about a general disregard and
disrespect of their neighbourhood by 'them' – 'them' could mean
the local government, all politicians, wealthy people, and all those
who did not live on council estates. 'Them' or 'they' often meant
people who were 'supposed' to help, such as the police; those who
were paid to work within the community but who did not live there
were especially resented.

The amount of drug use and drug dealing on the estate was the
issue that was constantly raised by the women, and something that

the women were extremely frustrated and angry about. When I spoke to Claire, who had described herself as a 'lifer', she described the normality of what, for many, might seem a severe crime and a frightening scenario:

> "The drugs … it's like the pied piper has come but it's a crack pipe and the kids are either selling it or using it, but probably they are using the crack to keep the badness away, maybe to support themselves to face the misery and deprivation that we have to live with, you see kids dealing as bright as day in front of me and where are the police? Just humble me can say that I have seen four crack deals go on … what are the people doing who are being paid to stop this? There's something not right here, they could have dealt with this years ago … yet they tell us they're there for us, but where are they? Maybe someone like me, a 'lifer' here in St Ann's, maybe I should get a job in the police force, I know what they're doing, get people who lived it and want it stopped in our streets, not kids from West Bridgford who have decided to be a police officer and then … horrified when they see four black guys standing there, they are frightened."

Louise told me that there were too many 'druggies' on the estate and this was the reason why there was so much crime; she also raised the issue again that St Ann's had been 'excluded' from the rest of Nottingham, that it was seen as and treated differently, and because of this, she felt disrespected by the rest of Nottingham:

> "I love it when people turn round to me and say, oh there's crime everywhere, crime in West Bridgford, I think, yeah, it's small compared to what we have here, it's tiny, and I think, yeah, come and live here then … I've seen my car smashed up, I've seen incidents on the street where I've had to have the police in to come, like fights on the street … police are always round here with helicopters."

However, Louise, who had lived in St Ann's all of her life with her family, and thought she was often viewed as 'rough and ready', did have another take on the situation when I asked her who the 'druggies' were:

> "No they aren't originals, they are people who have come from out of town or are homeless, they aren't the originals, I know quite a few lads at the bottom of the street and they're okay, but I think it's the outsiders coming in and bringing the badness with them."

Louise knew some of the 'shotters' (drug dealers) at the bottom of her street – they had gone to school with her daughter and she thought that they 'were alright'; she knew they were drug dealing but felt that it was not them who were causing the 'badness', as they were always respectful of her and her daughter. The residents within St Ann's knew and understood their estate, and were aware of the problems within it; what they did keep coming back to was how they were viewed and treated by 'others', and this treatment was constantly perpetuated and condoned because they were viewed as somehow different, deficient, or, as Louise said, 'rough and ready'.

It seems that 'being St Ann's' could work as a defence mechanism, to fend off those who 'looked down on St Ann's', so being an 'original' or 'a lifer' gave a person a certain amount of credibility, and respect at least, within the neighbourhood. The people who lived in this neighbourhood but who were viewed as 'outsiders' and 'not St Ann's', like the 'Iraqis' and the 'druggies', who behaved, acted and looked different from 'St Ann's', were not easily tolerated within the neighbourhood, and were often subject to aggression and violence by those who lived on the estate and who were classed as 'St Ann's'. The women also said that they advertised just how far St Ann's had fallen down the social ladder; as Lorraine said, "They put them here 'cos it's such a shit hole."

Although the men were angrier than the women about their personal circumstances, not being able to get 'good work' or being harassed by the police, they were less fatalistic about how bad the neighbourhood was. They understood it as territory, 'their territory', a place where they had some control over their lives, where they could walk, drive, dress and speak as they wished, although all recognised the constant 'war' with the police, who they felt were there to stop them doing what they wanted in their 'endz' (neighbourhood). The physical and social decline of the neighbourhood the women were experiencing through the closure of many services, and the general run-down look of the estate, did not affect the men in the same way.

As I have noted, the men at the gym and the barbers shop did not protect their profiles in the same ways as the women; they talked openly about how they made money, their time spent in jail, the problems they had with the police in the neighbourhood and their relationships with their girlfriends and babymothers. They had very little engagement with anyone from outside the neighbourhood, and minimum interaction with statuary services, benefit agencies and housing departments. Very few of the men I knew were registered with a GP, and most of them relied on their female networks, of mothers, daughters and girlfriends, to get them prescriptions or medication if they needed it. They talked to me about the constant cat-and-mouse games they played with the police, and that they knew "how to get around things": if you had no address and no name, the police couldn't find you, and they needed substantial evidence to search an address you did not live at. One of the men who sold cannabis from his home had mechanisms fitted to the outside door of his flat, which prevented the police from ram-raiding his front door off, and which gave him enough time to either get out of the flat or to 'flush' his stock. These were occupational hazards – drug dealing for some of the men and for some of the women was their business, it was how they 'got by', it was how they countered the precariousness of their lives, and it was employment. In addition to always having to be one step ahead of the police, the men also had the increasing problem of 'stop and search', especially the process of being pulled over in their cars as they drove around the estate. Many told me that being a black man with a car in St Ann's meant constant hassle from the police, to the extent that the men who were drug dealing or taking part in any illegal activity used local taxis to get around the estate to avoid being 'pulled by the feds'.

August 2011

I was approaching the end of my research with the men in St Ann's, and I had built up some really strong relationships with men like Tyler, Tony and Jerome through the gym and in the barbers shop. I felt I had a good understanding of the men's lives in St Ann's, and how they differed from the women's, and was thinking about how I would put all of this together in a book that would give an honest account of the neighbourhood. I was feeling quite positive about the book, and how I would represent the people and the neighbourhood. Policy Press, my publisher, had been really helpful and supportive, and I was ready to finish up with the men and to start to write. However, events took hold of my plans during August 2011 and subsequently changed many aspects to the research, the neighbourhood, and for many of the families included in this book.

When I first heard the news of the fatal shooting of Mark Duggan, a 29-year-old man from Tottenham, North East London, I was both interested and saddened – another young man lost, another life wasted, and another grieving family. This narrative was not unusual – we had witnessed and felt this type of loss of young men and women in Nottingham: Brendan Lawrence, a 16-year-old in 2002, Danielle Beccan, a 14-year-old in 2004, and others since who had died on our streets because of turf wars, arguments, accidents or anger. However, it was the events after Mark Duggan died in August 2011 that made his death notorious.

As I sat and watched the news unfold, and the story of Mark Duggan's death by a police marksman became more prominent in the running order, I was not surprised by the anger and frustration coming from this community in London. There was something about this anger that was an amalgamation of everything I had heard and witnessed over the previous eight years in my own community. The stress, the feeling of having no control over your own life, and the desperation of the powerless were being recounted by people on my television screen, but living in a different part of the country. I remember watching two young men being interviewed for Channel 4 News wearing bandanas over their faces in the middle of Tottenham, saying the same things I had heard in Nottingham – they were trying to explain to the news media through their anger and resentment the problems they were experiencing – constant police harassment, no jobs, no money, no one interested in them unless it was to demonise them, and believing that those in power wanted them 'wiped out'. This was all too familiar – I had heard it every day in the community centre, in the gym and in the barbers shop. I understood what was being said, but it was clear that the reporter did not. As events unfolded, the frustration and anger within Tottenham turned outwards and moved through the country like waves of anger and despair in similar neighbourhoods throughout English cities. Over the five days in August 2011 the civil unrest, burning and looting of buildings and rioting were shown around the world through extensive media coverage. Those incidences of civil unrest initiated widespread debates about English inner cities that focused on the morality, values and behaviour of those who lived within them. The riots resulted in a resurrection of the Conservative Party rhetoric of 'broken' Britain and, more notably, allowed and opened up space in English politics for the fear and loathing to return regarding 'the underclass'.

By 9 August, tension and fear had moved up the country, and I realised that in Nottingham there were people who wanted to become involved in the civil unrest and protest. I was in the city at about 3 o'clock in the afternoon, and most shops had been boarded up; the police were everywhere and private security guards stood outside some of the sports shops and phone shops. Nottingham city centre had effectively been 'locked off'; there were very few people around, and I hoped none of my family, friends and neighbours would go into the city later. The police and security guards had 'secured' the city and seemed very prepared. As I drove home I saw some of the men I knew on the Wells Road, the main road going through St Ann's; they were stood outside a fast food shop, and had not been in the gym that day. There were about 12 men that I recognised – they were agitated and didn't feel much like talking to me. I could usually have a laugh and a joke with them, but not today – they seemed uninterested in me, and wanted me to go. I didn't push it; I got back into my car and waved and went home.

My son arrived home from work at about 5 o'clock; he worked in a shop in the city centre and said they had closed up early on police advice. The police were locking off the city centre and wanted people out. My son was very happy about this – it had got him out of work early, and he hoped it would kick off around his workplace so he wouldn't have to go in the next day. After a brief conversation with his friend on the phone, he told me he was going out. I asked him where and why he was going out, and he told me that his friend was coming to pick him up in his car and they were going out to 'watch the riots'.

It is interesting how the shooting and death of a young man in London had managed to become so relevant in my home and with my son. I knew that my son could not go out on the streets that night; he was 22, mixed raced, and lived in St Ann's. I explained to him that he could not be out – the police would see him only as another black guy from St Ann's, a rioter, a gang member even. My son laughed at this – how would anyone think that about him? He worked in a shop in town, and looks like Phil Lynott from the 1970s rock band Thin Lizzy. He considers himself a 'hipster', not a gangster. However, I know what happens in times of civil unrest. I had been 16 in the miners' strike in 1984, and had experience of how the police manage 'civil unrest'. It seems to me – and it is common opinion among this local community or any communities affected by this – that the police arrest everyone for anything or nothing and think about it later, usually much later, through the pressure of public enquiries. I was listening to the rhetoric of the politicians and the media updates about what had been happening in other parts of the country during the unrest, and knew that any notions of fairness of the law and rationality in the country had gone and been replaced by vengeful anger towards those who were involved and out on the streets. I persuaded my son that he should stay in with me and watch the riots on the telly, like everyone else.

Within about an hour I began to receive messages on my Blackberry with updates from various contacts and neighbours about what was happening in Nottingham. There were updates on Facebook, with people posting what they could see out of their windows and what they had heard was happening. I was receiving updates about a group of men who were on the roof of the private school in Nottingham, and there were also messages coming through that a college had been set on fire, and there were about a hundred people gathered in one of the local parks. Later I read messages describing a police station on fire and youths stood outside throwing fire bombs at police cars. From inside my house I could hear police and other emergency vehicle sirens; the police helicopter was hovering low above the estate for most of the night (although that was a regular occurrence).

The next day I went to the gym, and it was alive with gossip and talk – who had heard what, who knew what, and who had been arrested. I learned that about six of the men I knew had been arrested the night before for 'rioting', and I heard many other stories about events that had taken place. Over the following days, the unrest throughout the country subsided, and the people who had been involved were being made examples of through the court system. The media, politicians and the 'common knowledge, common-sense rhetoric' in the following days and weeks was about 'thuggery', 'looting', 'criminality' and 'gangs'. Politicians were outraged, the media were outraged, middle England was outraged, and justice was being demanded through harsh and rushed sentencing of those who had supposedly been involved.

Over the following weeks I was contacted by several women I knew on the estate who wanted to talk to me about what had happened to their sons, and to ask my advice about how they could fight the charges their sons were facing. They contacted me because I think they didn't know who else might help, and they hoped that I would, or I would at least know someone who could. I visited Yvonne in October 2011. She was a single mum and worked part time at the University of Nottingham as a cleaner in the evenings. She had two children, 17-year-old Ayesha who was studying A-levels at a local sixth form college and hoped to get a place at the University of Nottingham, and Jerome, 14, who had been arrested for violent disorder during the disturbances in Nottingham. Jerome had been put on a tag (electronic tagging device), and his movements had been restricted by a curfew while the case against him was filed with the authorities. Yvonne was struggling with the judicial process – her family were now involved in because of her son's involvement in the riots. I interviewed Jerome about his arrest and then sat and had a coffee with Yvonne; she was not sleeping well, and was on anti-depressants:

"They keep asking me all the time where were you, why didn't you keep him [Jerome] in, you knew not to let him out, it had been on the telly all day, 'don't let your kids out', well, to be honest, Lisa, I was at work cleaning, what was I supposed to do, not go? I was sat on the bus coming back, it was stuck in traffic, I remember thinking what's going off now? I didn't know it was him [Jerome] getting arrested."

Yvonne then went on to tell me the problems she had been having since Jerome had been electronically tagged:

"Now I've got to go on parenting classes, well I'll tell you, I'm not going, I'm working and how do they expect me to keep him [Jerome] in the house from 6 at night until 8 in the morning, he's a 14-year-old lad, it's killing all of us, he's been on this order for four months now and unless he pleads guilty, it's on until April when the trial's scheduled, I can't have another four months of this."

Yvonne was at her wits end — she knew she had to go to work, but she also knew that someone had to stay in and make sure Jerome kept to his curfew, otherwise both of them would end up in jail. I really felt for her, she was desperate, and looked worn out with the stress of it. She told me that she had recently started to drink quite heavily late in the evenings because of the worry of what was happening to her family, and I knew that she was at breaking point.

I asked Jerome about his involvement the night he was arrested. He had gone to a local park with a group of older men who were respected on the estate through their ability to make money and their involvement in a local gang. The aim was to assemble a large group and to go into the city; they told Jerome they were 'going to get the police'. Jerome told me there were no plans to loot or steal anything — it was all about 'getting the police'. However, the police had intercepted them before they left the park, and had let the police dogs off the leads. Jerome was terrified of the dogs, and climbed up on to the school roof to get away from them, where he was arrested. I asked him about what had happened since. He told me he hated the curfew and the tag: he wanted to go out on the street with his mates, and he wanted to plead guilty to the charge in order to have the tag removed, but his mum didn't want him to. Jerome was very angry – he felt that being kept in the house virtually under house arrest for five months was unfair; he didn't think he had done anything wrong, although he was willing to plead guilty for anything in order to get the tag removed. I asked him what the riots had been about and he said "It's about money, nothing else matters, if you have got money no one cares who you are." He looked up to his dad who was 'on road' (drug dealing). This 14-year-old in St Ann's knew and recognised the respect and status that came with this local position; he wanted to be respected, he wanted to feel valued, and knew that his social position outside the estate, unless he had money, was of no value. I asked Jerome what he wanted to do when he left school. His answer was simple – 'entrepreneur' – he wanted to be "rich like Alan Sugar". I asked him about politics and what he knew about some of the problems people were experiencing in Britain because of the government's cuts. Jerome said he had heard about a 'credit crunch' and wasn't sure how it affected his mum; he knew in the last year that they could no longer afford real Coca Cola, and now had to have "the crap stuff".

After speaking to Jerome I went back into the kitchen and sat with Yvonne a bit longer; she had drunk several cans of strong lager and was becoming incoherent. Her daughter Ayesha came in and started shouting at her mother about her getting drunk again, and I wondered whether this young woman would actually make it to the University of Nottingham as a psychology student in light of the turmoil at home.

Kath and Perry

Kath contacted me a few months after the riots. I received an email where she outlined the problems she was having with the judicial system since her son Perry had been arrested and had subsequently been remanded in jail on 9 August 2011. One of the police officers investigating Perry's case had passed on my details – he had apparently heard me on the radio talking about the riots, and about the community in Nottingham. He then found an article I had written and suggested I might be able to offer some support. I went on to meet and talk to this police officer in St Ann's about some of the problems the neighbourhood was having with policing, and in actual fact he was empathetic, especially around the policy of stop and search, and the pulling over of black men driving around the estate. He knew there were problems, but, like many police officers on the front line, he did not know what he could do about it. Like many police officers I have spoken to over the years about community policing and government cuts, he recognised that his job was getting more difficult and complex, moving into social care and social work, something that was not compatible with law enforcement.

So following the police officer's advice, Kath contacted me and I met her at her home. She presented me with hundreds and hundreds of documents relating to her son, Perry's, case. Perry was 20 when he was arrested, a young lad from St Ann's not that much unlike my own son. He worked in a phone shop in the city centre and had never been in trouble with the police until 9 August 2011, when he was arrested on the charge of violent disorder, along with two other men on a street in Nottingham. The trial had gone through quite quickly, and in May 2012 Perry was found guilty and sentenced to three years in prison along with the two other men.

When I met Kath she was angry and upset, and in shock; it was a few days after the sentencing and she did not believe that her son would have been found guilty. She thought at every point since August 2011 that he would be freed and the police would realise it had been a big mistake.

Perry had gone to the gym on the morning of 9 August 2011, and then went to work in the city centre. He, like my son, had finished work early because of the fear of looting in the city, and he went home to St Ann's. At about 7 o'clock Perry decided to go out and get some food from the takeaway on the main road that was near the private school. After buying his food he thought he would go and have a look at what was happening in the neighbourhood; there were police vans everywhere and he was, as we say in St Ann's, being 'farce' (nosey), another Jamaican word that is commonly and widely used on the estate. As Perry stood at the top of one of the streets, about 10 youths came running past him, and he saw a number of police officers in riot gear with dogs following. He realised he was in the way and panicked and started to run. Perry was arrested with two other men, neither of whom he knew. He was remanded to prison, as were all the men who had been arrested that night, until his trial that was five months away. He was remanded because he was over 18, whereas Jerome had been tagged because he was only 14.

Perry was found guilty of violent disorder and sentenced to three years in jail. The main argument of the prosecution was that Perry had been on the street in order to 'get up to no good', otherwise why else would he have been there? Another part of the prosecution's argument was that Perry was wearing a red bandana, which, they argued, was a signifier that Perry was part of a gang in St Ann's. This line of defence seemed to go along way with the jurors, even though there was no evidence that Perry had done anything apart from being on the street that night, and he looked like a rioter. The police went through Perry's phone records and contacts – he was not in contact with anyone else who had been arrested that night, and the police admitted that he didn't seem to know anyone else who he had been arrested with. But among the furore about the riots, and the rising fear of 'the underclass' and inner-city 'gangs', 12 men and women from Nottingham believed that Perry was a 'rioter'.

Kath was a tough woman but was heartbroken that her son, her boy, was in a big man's prison; she was scared for him and was desperate to get him home. When I met Kath and heard about Perry, this story struck me and greatly affected me. I knew what was happening to them could just as easily be happening to me and my son. Perry was found guilty despite the police having no evidence that he had done anything wrong that night, apart from being a young black man and being outdoors on 9 August 2011. He could have been out on the same street the night before and nothing would have happened, or the night after. Kath and Perry have tried to fight his conviction through the Court of Human Rights on the basis that the collective element of 'violent disorder' is unfair. Perry's legal representation has stated that:

> There are a number of people whose convictions are dubious
> because they have really good explanations for being there. They
> have no past criminal record. And they have been convicted
> because there was a collective element about the offence which
> trapped them. (BBC News Nottingham, 2012)

Over the last two years I have got to know Kath really well, and I
have been to several events with her where we have raised Perry's
case, and tried to get support for challenging what Kath believes is
his wrongful arrest. It has been difficult, and although there have
been sympathies for Kath, there has been very little practical support
available for her and Perry to fight this.

Perry was released from prison in 2013. What he wants now is to
be able to just get on with his life and to put this episode of arrest
and prison behind him. He has refused to continue with the fight
to clear his name and to overturn his conviction; he has had enough
and he wants to live a normal life, hopefully going back to work at
some point, although both Kath and Perry realise this is going to
be extremely difficult because of his conviction and because of the
way the 2011 August riots are remembered in the public psyche.

I still speak to Kath quite often; we exchange messages on Facebook
and text each other. What has happened to Kath and her family has
had a profound effect on all of them, and the devastating effects of
Perry's arrest and incarceration on Kath and the rest of her family
have not lessened over time.

Duggan verdict: 'lawful killing'

The inquest of Mark Duggan's death took over four weeks to
conclude, and in early January 2014, a statement was made outside
the Royal Courts of Justice in Central London that by a majority of
eight to two, the jury found that the 2011 shooting was lawful, and
that the police had acted lawfully when they shot Mark Duggan in
Tottenham. However, by the same eight to two majority, they believed
that Mark Duggan did not have a gun in his hand when the police
surrounded him; the jury surmised that he 'threw' it from the taxi
he was travelling in when armed police forced it to stop.

The verdict on Mark Duggan's death is as significant as the day he was killed. Twelve ordinary men and women living in London had come to a conclusion that, even though Mark Duggan was not any threat to the police the moments before he was shot and killed, the police were lawful in their actions. I do not know how they came to that decision – only the 12 people involved will know that. However, the consequences are both far-reaching and frightening. Since 2011 Mark Duggan's family and his life have been under constant media spotlight – reports of his 'gangster lifestyle' and his family's connections to organised crime in other parts of the UK have been widespread. Richard Littlejohn in the *Mail Online* wrote an article about the Duggan inquest two days after the verdict on 10 January 2014, where he launched into a vicious attack on the Duggan family, in particular Pamela Duggan, Mark's grieving mother:

> She looked like Vicky Pollard's granny and spoke in a curious hybrid accent, a cross between Ali G and Liam Gallagher of Oasis. Manc meets Jafaican.

> Carole Duggan, with her severe "council estate face-lift" swept-back hairdo, could have wandered off the set of Channel 4's Benefits Street after a session in the boozer with "White Dee" and "Black Dee". (Littlejohn, 2014)

In his article, Richard Littlejohn played with every stereotype and stigmatisation the men and women in St Ann's have to cope with and complain about on a daily basis. Throughout this book I have shown how stigma and stereotype are both pervasive and damaging. The Duggan verdict shows clearly that, even though Mark Duggan was perceived to be no actual threat at the time of the shooting, the police were entitled to have:

> ... an honest-held belief that he was in imminent danger of him and his colleagues being shot. (Owen, 2014)

The point here is that the jury members accepted that this young man, mixed race, from Tottenham, was 'potentially dangerous', an unknown threat, and consequently enough of a threat that the police were justified in shooting an unarmed man and killing him on the streets of London.

The day that this verdict was announced, and the following days when the vile rhetoric about the Duggan family reignited the media and the public's desire to loathe and ridicule those who may or may not have been involved in the civil unrest in 2011, but perhaps 'look' and 'act' like they might have, Kath, Perry's mum, sent me these messages:

> Grrrr ... just another middle class, powerful ... unconscious, corrupt, inhumane, unjust FINGER up at us again, Lisa. What they hoping for next? another riot? In order to have an excuse (not that they need any) to manhandle, set up, target, arrest ... and ultimately "lock up" the rest of our youth. The ones they didn't manage to "rid our streets and communities of the last time around"? Bet their favourite film is "The Purge"! That'll be their next move, hun. Hope you're well. Stay safe. "And BE HEARD"! XX

Kath then went on to say how this decision has made her frightened for her children and other people's children:

> Lisa, hun. I wake up every day frightened for my boys ... and all the others. Their mothers. And families out there. Always anxious that they got to where they were going safely. Got back safely. And that's just "going shop". Unless we get through to our children. Because no matter how old they are ... they are "always that to us" ... and we are having to watch over them, and fret as if they are still little because of the dangers facing them 24/7. It's a sad day when the only time you feel they "are safe" is when they are "under our roofs" ... with us! Doesn't look hopeful that we look forward to them "spreading their wings" ... enjoying adventures, travel, families of their own. They have got to realise "once and for all" that they are NOT EACH OTHER'S ENEMY ... the SYSTEM is the enemy. And unless we all pull together to say "We're not having it anymore.... THIS ALL STOPS NOW" ...

then we will see our beautiful cultures ... our beautiful children "just fade from society" all together! Just as planned!! Xxx

And then she went on to say how thankful she was to me for supporting her, and how this period in her life and her children's lives may never be over:

It's far from over Lisa. What happened has determined the rest of his life for the foreseeable future. And "changed him". I will never forget your selfless support hun ... and always remember you saying "that could have easily been your son". The fact that it "wasn't" would have been all far too many people would have been interested in ... or cared about. But not you, sweet lady. You're not one of those people that only decide to "raise awareness" to a cause due to personally being affected by something. Pity this awful world "that some of us live in" doesn't have more Lisa Mckenzies. And I will hold our day spent together at Your Uni fondly in my memories. Xxx

Kath's reaction as a mother whose children fitted the description of the stereotyped and stigmatised image of the 'dangerous working class' was that of fear, shock, disbelief and sadness. My reaction was exactly the same – like many mothers of young black and mixed-race young men, I realise that Britain is a far more dangerous place for our children than it was prior to the shooting of Mark Duggan. The fear of the young black, or mixed-race, man, and the loathing for the families who live on council estates, have been institutionalised and legitimated through the courts and our legal system.

The courts convicted those who took part in the 2011 English riots, and along with most of the British public have judged along with the mainstream media, and almost all of our mainstream politicians, that those who were part of the civil unrest were 'morally bankrupt' and 'feral'. Right-wing journalist Max Hastings, in the *Daily Mail*, wrote of these and other men involved the riots: 'Their behaviour on the streets resembled that of the polar bear which attacked a Norwegian tourist camp. They were doing what came naturally and, unlike the bear, no one even shot them for it' (Hastings, 2011).

Prime Minister David Cameron argued in his speech following the riots a week later, that 'The riots were not about race, government cuts or poverty. They were about behaviour', and although England had seen some 'sickening acts', the big society was working through the 'Best of British' with the clean-up operation #riotcleanup in Tottenham where the local community came out and cleared the streets with their own brooms (BBC News Nottingham, 2012). These comments from media and political discourse are neither surprising nor shocking; neither was the level of crime, anger and violence on the streets during that first week in August 2011. There has been a gradual exclusion, devaluing and stigmatisation of sections of the British working class for several generations. I have noted over eight years through the narratives of those who live in St Ann's the feelings of powerlessness and the rage that comes out of this level of despair, and that consequently the community turns in on itself. The residents of poor communities look inwards for sanctuary; they find it locally, with the unintended consequences of causing damage both to themselves and to their communities.

Imogen Tyler, in her recent book *Revolting subjects* (2013), notes that during the week of the August 2011 riots in England the term 'scum' was commonly used in all print and news media, not only about those who were taking part in the rioting, but also their families, communities, and what was often referred to as 'the scum class'. The language of the 'underclass' and the 'culture of poverty' had been reclaimed and was being reused by those who had been gearing up for some time to justify cuts to public services, welfare benefits, and the general rolling back of the state. The 2011 riots, and then the legitimate justification of the murder of a young man who may or may not have been involved in gangs/drugs/guns but who was definitely from a poor working-class family, served and was used as 'definitive proof' of a group or class of people that have been defined and known by their anti-social and destructive behaviour.

The death of Mark Duggan in 2011, and then the verdict at the inquest in 2014, shows clearly that the stigma and stereotype of the working class, of the council estate family and of the poor is more far-reaching than simply 'being looked down on'. I can only see that this verdict legitimises and legalises violence by those in power towards the poor.

Last words:
the working class – a sorry state?

From the accounts written in this book it might be easy to surmise that the British working class are in a sorry state; known and represented as 'lacking' and 'deficit', they struggle to find work, constantly fight with social services in order to maintain any type of decent existence, sell drugs, dodge the police, and are eventually filled with so much anger and frustration that they turn their anger on each other and within their own communities. They are known and named as feral, underclass, scum, and living on 'Benefits Street'. This book may appear as a depressing account of contemporary life in Britain. However, from the beginning, I explained this that was a complex story, filled with complex narratives from people who manage to 'get by' despite the inherent structural problems that unequal Britain bestows on them. Some of those problems are the way the people in this book, the poorest 10 per cent of the population, and those who live in this council estate in Nottingham, are seen and known by the rest of the British population.

Narratives are important – the ways that narratives are constructed about different groups affect their life chances, and also in the ways these groups see themselves. In recent years there has been a clear and definite return to the imagery of the 'underclass', with council estates representing a modern version of Hogarth's Gin Lane. This version is clear and has characters who are recognisable – the dangerous and violent gang member and the welfare-absorbing single mother. The discourses that surround these characters are their assumed lack of common societal values and morality, and their wilful self-destruction. It is their self-destructive behaviour, through their own practices, tastes, what they wear, how they speak and who they decide to share their beds with that begins to represent a real threat to British values and national life, with seemingly the only rational answer that this danger to British society coming from below must be curbed through punitive measures – benefits cuts – reawakening the whole 'deserving versus undeserving' debate.

What I have also shown throughout this book, through the narratives and the stories that people have told me about themselves and their community, is that local narratives linked to local identities are important. The people who live in the St Ann's estate in Nottingham believe they have something special, something that is to be envied, and something that has kept at bay the onslaught of the various political parties, institutions and policies, which have, over at least one generation, undermined and attempted to dismantle what it means to be and to live in a working-class community. The contrast and complexity to this story of the British working class amazes me, and makes me proud, and is as binary as any opposites can be. I remember walking under one of the underpasses that links the estate together under a main road, walking through the litter-strewn concrete subway, covered in graffiti (and not the type of artistic or clever graffiti you might see in Bristol, Brighton or in Shoreditch). As you walk you have to watch your feet and look at the floor, because you don't want to step into dog shit, at the same time keeping an eye on what is happening around you – it is, after all, a dark subterranean alley reminiscent of a scene from Stanley Kubrick's interpretation of *A clockwork orange*. Walking through this subterranean part of the city your senses pick up on the dog shit, the litter, the graffiti, and also the overwhelming smell of stale piss, but you come out the other end, you see the light, literally at the end of the tunnel, and you head for it.

I remember emerging one day from this underpass to the smell of washing powder, the overwhelming smell of clean washing. At the backs of the houses on this windy day, and in the small square back yards, were rows of large, white, clean and fresh smelling sheets. The contrast was overwhelming, and it is this contrast that symbolises the story I wanted to tell, the difference between stale piss and clean washing, side by side. This is the complexity of the people's lives who live on this council estate in Nottingham. And it is this constant battle to overcome the difficulties that working-class people have to endure that keeps them going, gives them their compassion, their humour, and their sense of who they are, something I see as to be envied by those on the outside who do not recognise the St Ann's way of life. I also see resentment because St Ann's residents are proud of their community and their way of life when, as those on the outside see it, they have no right to be. Being part of a community, the sense of belonging and the strong sense of who you are, is often lost in contemporary Britain. What I have shown in this book is that this can still be found within the council estates and among the people who need and recognise community as important to their well-being. As they battle between the narratives created about them linked to 'broken' Britain, their self-exclusion and their 'underclass' status, they tell their own narratives of local identity and community, pride, and the importance of belonging. However, even these small but central victories and acts of resistance within council estates are undermined, along with the hope of a future that includes family stability, somewhere to live and to make plans, and work that pays a decent living wage.

The women and the men on the estate have formed very strong family and kinship bonds with each other for stability. Despite the many discussions, and hand-wringing sentiments, particularly from the middle class in the UK that 'community is in crisis' and that people no longer feel connected to their neighbours, family, kinship and community are still important for men and women in order to 'get by'. The men conduct their lives out of necessity in the shadows of the estate, while the women live under the harsh spotlight and judgement of 'the officials'.

Anger was a natural response to many of the difficult daily interactions within this neighbourhood – the women often responded to the constant interrogation with raised voices, frustration and sometimes depression. The men had constant problems with the police, and distrusted all 'officials', having as little contact as possible, which often made family life stressful and difficult. Despite this, there was a strong sense of community, a pride among this population because of who they were, and the hardships they knew they had to endure. They were extremely proud of their 'mixing', talking about their knowledge of racism, and why it was wrong and not tolerated in this community – they talked about this sense of openness to other people coming in as something special, and they knew other communities and other people would struggle with what they had to put up with, which they had turned into something 'special' about them and their community.

Even though there were clearly problems in this community, which I believe I have outlined in detail, these were rarely caused by those who lived here, but rather by the thoughtlessness of others, and sometimes, as the residents suspected, because of purposeful prejudice and disrespect for them.

I am often asked what policy interventions are needed to 'change' or to 'help' 'these people' – apparently I am now an expert. There was a point when I tried to answer this question, with helpful suggestions, better resources, more resources, training, employment, skills, decent housing and respect. Although all of these things are important, and all of these things are needed, I have to ask whether these things are actually possible in this current climate of winner takes all and the irrationality of the open market, a game that is fixed from the beginning. Policy interventions within poor neighbourhoods are usually inadequate. They often position poor neighbourhoods and their residents without worth and value, the deficit model of a community and a group of people constantly lacking in what is needed to be 'successful citizens', focusing on changing the behaviours of poor people in order to change neighbourhoods. These types of prescriptive and 'one size fits all' measures lack the understanding that within poor communities there are real complexities and nuances, just like the ones demonstrated throughout this book. The local value systems, what is valued within, and what is important to those who live in poor neighbourhoods, their practices, their taste, and how they want to live their lives – these have meaning to those within that community, although they are often misunderstood, disrespected and not recognised by those on the outside, leading to notions that poor people and poor neighbourhoods are without any value at all.

In recognising this complexity, it would be wrong within this conclusion to extend these findings into more 'off the cuff' policy recommendations; instead, the aim is to provide alternative ways of thinking about poor communities and their residents.

From the outset I have maintained that this is a complex account of a council estate and working-class life within it. There are inconsistencies, contradictions and a constant but restless dynamic in the stories and the practices that make up council estate life for the people involved in this research. The aim at the beginning of this process was to challenge the negative and homogeneous readings of Britain's council estates and their residents, the rhetoric of 'the underclass', and the Conservative notion of a 'broken Britain' and troubled families with only 'troubled' families to blame.

Positive namings

From the outset I have examined and shown how the poor working class have been named, understood and recognised within public discourse, and how those namings inform policy, the wider British public and poor working-class people themselves. I have argued that there is a lack of positive namings and valuations of working-class practices and behaviours, and that the poor working class have become sites of ridicule and condemnation.

There have been many attempts to 'fix' the problems of the poor. New Labour's attempt at understanding social exclusion failed. It moved away from its original form, which was about the multidimensional effects of poverty, including a lack of resources, but also broadened out to include how social structures had become broken down within a society, and how specific groups became excluded from having any political power or the resources to make changes to their own lives. Instead New Labour continued on the easy and populist path, which was about changing people, changing communities and changing cultures, rather than changing structures, and the unfair, and unequal, game of the open market. Consequently the focus moved from 'exclusion' to 'the excluded', to specific neighbourhoods and their residents – so the neighbourhood 'suffered' from social exclusion and the residents became 'the excluded'. They became known and named, stigmatised because of where they lived, and their practices and behaviours became scrutinised as problems within themselves, rather than methods for managing the difficult situations they encountered.

These arguments regarding the places where the poor live and their behaviour and practices being to blame for all social ills are not new. I would like to say that these arguments are new and ground-breaking, but they are not, which makes them all the more poignant. Michael Young and Peter Willmott (2007 [1957]) found similar practices within London's East End in the early 1950s. Oscar Lewis (1961) also argued that local value systems were used within poor neighbourhoods in Mexico City to compensate for what was not available; his theory of the culture of poverty was then used by neoliberal politicians to blame the poor for their poverty by focusing only on behaviour while ignoring the conditions in which they had to live. The original St Ann's study during the 1960s, by Coates and Silburn, also highlighted residents' coping strategies, but the research focused on the poor conditions in which the residents lived and also the low wages they received for full-time manual work. They argued that these were the real problems within the neighbourhood (Coates and Silburn, 1970). Even then, they still had to counter the arguments that arose, that St Ann's residents were buying televisions and smoking cigarettes when they should have been spending their money on more 'worthy' things. It seems incredible that today, in 2015, this research has added to that list, again highlighting the difficult conditions in which the poor are living, and still having to make the argument that to focus solely on the behaviour of the poor is both misplaced and cruel.

The second part to this argument is how the poor working class, those without regular and stable employment, those who are low paid, and those with very little formal education, are now known and named as 'troubled', 'broken' 'shirkers' who contribute nothing to society, despite evidence from Tracy Shildrick and colleagues who have shown clearly in their work that it is the 'low pay, no pay' cycle that is crippling and disabling poor communities and families (Shildrick et al, 2012). I have argued that over the last 30 years, because of how capitalism has changed the social conditions within poor working-class neighbourhoods, the poor working class in particular have become devalued. Their traditional places of employment have gone, and they are now existing on the outside of a modern Britain.

There has, however, been a shift in class positioning within the UK, possibly in an attempt to remove it from the British consciousness. Nancy Fraser (1997), Bev Skeggs (1997, 2004, 2009) Valerie Walkerdine, Helen Lucey and June Melody (2001), have all written about the particularly difficult nature of theorising class as a concept. There have been recent arguments and discussions in academic circles and throughout the media that social class is no longer a useful concept, that the British population see themselves in other ways. Consequently, with the lack of social mobility and the widening gap of inequality, what is actually happening within the UK is that, rather than class becoming less important and less visible, there are sections of the population that are now being defined and known through a sharp and clear lens, whereby they can be easily identified, through their practices, their clothing, where they live, and 'who they are'.

Local inclusion

It is hardly surprising, therefore, that those who live in poor neighbourhoods and who are identified as the shirkers, the underclass or the broken, begin to recognise themselves through the mainstream discourse that defines them. Throughout this book I have asked what have been the consequences for those who live on the St Ann's council estate in Nottingham being known as valueless and deficit? Are they aware of the stigmatised readings regarding their lives? Throughout the narratives there has been a clear message – the people who live on this estate know and are fully aware that they are 'looked down on', they are 'made to feel small' and they are 'disrespected'. They talked about those negative namings and shame that is attached to claiming welfare benefits, living on council estates and being a single parent, struggling to find work.

The women in this research have a clear awareness of how they are known, particularly when it comes to the services that are on offer for them within their neighbourhood. They are aware of what happens to their profile when they use these services – they know that claiming benefits and living in social housing costs them dearly, in how they are viewed, and treated, within society, but they know they have to 'take it on the chin' in order to survive, to 'get by'. The women were acutely aware of 'never being good enough', and angry that their situation was, as they said, 'dire'. They discussed the ways they were demeaned and 'taken the piss out of' by those paid to work in the neighbourhood, they raged at how they were misrepresented within the media, ridiculed, laughed at and hated. They were also hurt by these representations, and often said it made them 'weak'. They knew that when all of these positions were lumped together with their 'mixed-race' children, they were classed, racialised and sexualised.

Both the men and women knew how those on the 'outside' viewed them, and subsequently treated them, so they looked inwards towards the estate, their families, friends and their wider community. They found value from within, and the resources within the estate became ever more valuable to them. Although the resources valued within this social group have no real exchange value outside of this social group, they are often recognised between similar people living in similar conditions. The people on the estate discussed this through their 'taste' in clothing, how they styled their hair, and especially through the amount of gold jewellery they wore, which was highly valued within the estate, but ridiculed outside. There were other valuable resources within the estate – the estate itself held worth, as being part of it, understanding the local culture, and being part of the networks inside offered resources and value to the community. 'Being St Ann's' was valued, and accumulating the resources to 'be

St Ann's' was an achievable goal. Although those resources, practices and culture marked the women, they became more distinguishable as council estate mothers. Such practices create a boundary around the outside, but at the same time create an inside, including and excluding.

Value

There are practices, resources and processes that the residents recognised within, making up the local value system. Motherhood had real value for the women; all without exception told me that the only thing they really felt proud of were their children. Being part of St Ann's, belonging to the community, was also important – most of the men and women spent much of their time in the neighbourhood. The women often worked voluntarily and unofficially within the community, although they were rarely acknowledged for the work they did. The men lived precarious lives, working in unstable and part-time employment, often relying on the underground economy for stability.

The local culture has been heavily influenced by black Jamaican culture, particularly for the mothers in this research whose children were mixed race, although this was not exclusive to them. Many of the other St Ann's residents, regardless of their ethnicity, also valued this culture; West Indian food, music and styles of dressing and ways of speaking were popular and embodied what 'being St Ann's' meant. Being authentic to the neighbourhood, being known and fitting in were other elements to how you became a person of value on the estate, but also to whom and how you were connected to the estate was equally important. The networks were complex, and the social hierarchies on the estate fed into the local value system – West Indian families were respected, and there were very few of the white working-class or West Indian families on the estate who did not have mixed-race relatives. Consequently, 'mixing' was also valued; as one of the women told me, "All this mixing is good for us … we are not white and boring now."

The men valued themselves through their 'masculinity', their ability to make money, to out-wit the police, and by being known and respected within the neighbourhood, protecting their territory as necessary.

Belonging and identification

There are several themes that run throughout this book – value and exclusion, and how those who live on this estate know themselves, recognise themselves and imagine themselves. When welfare policy sets out to name and change those it sees as failures, it has an impact on how the wider population sees those people, and also how those people see themselves. The negative namings, stigmatised readings and shame that are attached to claiming welfare benefits and living on council estates not only identify these groups as 'different' and 'lacking', but also allow these groups to internalise this general level of disrespect. However, it would be wrong to think that they only know themselves as 'valueless' – they do find value locally, in the local value system. In my academic work I have used Pierre Bourdieu's concept of 'habitus' to help me to understand how negative namings and stigmatised positions can be absorbed into an identity. Habitus can be historical and reference back to the understandings of social positions. It can also adapt, therefore it is not determining, but generative; it can help us to see how individuals and groups can push against, resist or adapt to those negative namings. As I have argued, the poor working class in St Ann's had experienced a devaluing of their social positions, but they did find value for themselves within their local culture, even though, by engaging within the local culture and 'being St Ann's', it further devalued their social position outside the estate. They found an identity within that they valued, even though it may not be understood as a mainstream valued identity.

'Being St Ann's' has many meanings and values attached to it; it offers a certain amount of safety through being known and 'fitting in'. However, there are other issues that 'being St Ann's' entails. In her book *Estates*, Lynsey Hanley talks about 'estatism', which is what happens when the council estate where you live seeps into your soul – you belong to it, it belongs to you. 'Estatism' is feelings, understandings and meanings that offer value, respect and worth to those who cannot achieve this, or believe they cannot, in any other place than where they live and among the people with whom they live together.

I have purposefully talked about pizza deliveries, milkmen and taxis — these are the small stories. I wanted to show the general disrespect and annoyance that life can be like for those who live on council estates, but again, I purposefully introduced the 'big stories' — of gang culture, drugs, guns and 'estatism'. In its present form the drug economy on the estate is relatively new, but the conditions in St Ann's that have allowed its success are not. The people who live in poor neighbourhoods, who come from poor families, and who have very little of the universally accepted and respected resources allowing a person to become valued, can become resentful, angry and suspicious — the cheery common folk whistling while making a virtue out of necessity really only exist in the post-war Ealing comedies.

What does exist here, in Nottingham, and within communities across the UK, where the poorest people live, are hardships caused by the consequences of structural inequality, a political system that does not engage those who have the least power, disenfranchisement relating to the notion of fairness regarding their families and their communities. However, there is also humour, love and care for their families, and within the wider community, a strong sense of identity and a belief that their strength and pride belongs in their local community, out of which it was born.

Afterword

'Austerity' has defined British political debate since the end of 2008, when the Conservatives abruptly abandoned their support for Labour's spending levels and constructed a new narrative that the country had been plunged into disaster by overspending. In the 'age of austerity', the nation's books were to be balanced on the backs of working, disabled and unemployed people. By 2014 – in the aftermath of the weakest economic recovery since the Victorian era – the Conservative-led coalition government was lauding the return of economic growth as vindication of its assault on public spending. But while it certainly was boom time for the rich – the *Sunday Times* Rich List recorded a doubling of the wealth of the richest 1,000 Britons between 2009 and 2014 – working people suffered the longest fall in living standards in well over a century. Disabled people faced the slashing of benefits, and the indignity and stress of appealing to win back their desperately needed support; workers enduring plummeting pay packets had their in-work benefits cut in real-terms; while no private pensions, no paid leave or no set hours became the reality for workers driven into zero-hour contracts or bogus self-employment.

And yet, as working-class Britain was expected to pay for a crisis caused by powerful elites, the voices of those punished by austerity were all but airbrushed from existence. No wonder: according to a government report published in August 2014, over half of the top 100 media professionals are privately educated, while the number of working-class MPs shrinks with every general election. The rise of unpaid internships and the weakening of trade unions and local government have helped turn the media and political worlds into closed shops for the privileged, ensuring that working-class voices are ever harder to come by. That's why a book like this is so important: because it allows intentionally ignored people to speak on their own terms about their experiences and their lives.

It is not simply that large swathes of Britain have been airbrushed out of existence, of course. What is even more convenient for the defenders of austerity is that the reality of life for many Britons has been replaced by demonised caricatures. Newspapers relentlessly hunt down unsympathetic, extreme examples of, say, unemployed people or immigrants, presenting them in terms that are intended to make their readers' blood boil. In modern Britain, it is the behaviour of those living in poverty that is relentlessly scrutinised, criticised and attacked. Those responsible for Britain's plight – whether it be bankers, tax-dodging corporations and wealthy individuals, or poverty-pay employers – are, relatively speaking, spared. Tensions in working-class communities have been ruthlessly exploited, with the object of making often struggling people envy each other: low-paid workers against the unemployed; private sector workers against public sector workers; those living here already against immigrants.

Little wonder, then, that Britons estimate that an average of 27 per cent of social security spending is lost to fraud (the government's own estimate is 0.7 per cent);[1] or that polls reveal that people dramatically over-estimate what benefits are worth or how long they are claimed for on average. But a counterblast of accurate statistics will not transform popular attitudes. It will surely be granting a platform to the otherwise ignored or demonised – allowing them to speak on their own terms – that will be most effective.

Demonisation and airbrushing long predates austerity, of course. Thatcherism promoted the idea that poverty and unemployment were individual failings, rather than social problems. If that was true, then the welfare state merely existed to subsidise the workshy, when really they should be forced to stand on their own two feet. Aspiration was recast as becoming middle class, leaving those who failed to do so somehow deemed as failures. But this book provides compelling examples, too, of the impact this has on the individual: of the 'symbolic violence' of the poorest working-class people being belittled, patronised and demonised.

Inequality is profoundly irrational as well as unjust. A dramatic concentration of wealth and power in so few hands while – in one of the most prosperous countries that has ever existed – hundreds of thousands are driven to food banks just to survive. It means billions of pounds of public money spent each year to subsidise wages that are otherwise all but impossible to live on. Such inequality has to be rationalised: and demonisation is a crucial element of this process. Those at the top deserve to be there because they are the most talented or able; those at the bottom are there because they are feckless and stupid. Inequality is implicitly justified as a fair reflection of people's talents, abilities and work ethics.

If a different sort of society is to be built – one run in the interests of those who keep society ticking, rather than a glorified racket for the privileged – then it will be created by people of goodwill in positions of power. The history of our country – the Tolpuddle Martyrs, the Chartists, the suffragettes, the labour movement, movements against sexism, racism and homophobia – tell us that change happens through people organising from below. One day, the 'hardships caused by the consequences of structural inequality', as the book puts it, will be abolished. But books that cast light on the difficult and all too ignored realities of modern Britain will surely play their part on bringing that day ever closer.

Owen Jones
London, November 2014

[1] 'Support for benefit cuts dependent on ignorance, TUC-commissioned poll finds', TUC press release, 2 January 2013.

Bibliography

Back, L. (1996) *New ethnicities and urban culture: Racisms and multi-culture in young lives*, London: Routledge.

Bart, L. (1962) 'It's a fine life' [song from the musical 'Oliver!'].

BBC News (2005) 'Children's names "spell trouble"', 23 September (http://news.bbc.co.uk/1/hi/education/4274318.stm).

BBC Newsnight (2003) 'Inner city gangs', BBC Two, 25 November.

BBC News Nottingham (2012) 'Nottingham riots: Perry Atherton prepares human rights case', 6 August (www.bbc.co.uk/news/uk-england-nottinghamshire-19148075).

Bourdieu, P. (1977) *Outline of a theory of practice*, Cambridge: Cambridge University Press.

Bourdieu, P. (1986) *Distinction: A critique of the social judgement of taste*, London: Routledge.

Bourdieu, P. (1990) *The logic of practice*, Cambridge: Polity.

Bourdieu, P. (2003) *Firing back: Against the tyranny of the market 2*, London, Verso.

Bourdieu P. and Wacquant L. (1992) *An invitation to reflexive sociology*, Cambridge: Polity.

Bourdieu, P. et al (1999) *The weight of the world: Social suffering in contemporary society*, Cambridge: Polity.

Cameron, D. (2011) 'English riots: David Cameron blames the parents for the mayhem', *Daily Record*, 15 August (www.dailyrecord.co.uk/news/uk-world-news/english-riots-david-cameron-blames-1109491).

Cameron, D. (2011) Speech delivered on BBC News, 12 August.

Charlesworth, S.J. (2000) *A phenomenology of working-class experience*, Cambridge: Cambridge University Press.

Coates, K. and Silburn, R. (1970) *Poverty: The forgotten Englishmen*, London: Penguin Books.

Coates, K. and Silburn, R. (1980) *Beyond the bulldozer*, Nottingham: Spokesman Books.

Collins, M. (2004) *The likes of us: A biography of the white working class*, London: Granta.

Cribb, J., Hood, A., Joyce, R. and Phillips, D. (2013) *Living standards, poverty and inequality in the UK: 2013*, London: Institute for Fiscal Studies.

CSJ (Centre for Social Justice) (2006) *Breakdown Britain*, London: CSJ.

Curtis, L.A. (1985) *American violence and public policy*, New Haven, CT and London: Yale University Press and Routledge.

Dorling, D. (2010) *Injustice*, Bristol: Policy Press.

Duncan-Smith, I. (2008) 'Broken ghettos', *The Times*, 30 November.

DWP (Department for Work and Pensions) (2004) *Nottingham City strategy – Business plan*, Draft, London: HMSO.

DWP (2008) *Opportunity, employment and progressions: Making skills work*, London: HMSO.

DWP (2008) *Raising expectations and increasing support: Reforming welfare for the future*, Cm 750, London: HMSO.

DWP (2009) *Unleashing aspiration*, London: HMSO.

DWP (2009) *Welfare Reform Bill 2009: No-one written off: Reforming welfare to reward responsibility*, Cm 7363, London: HMSO.

Eames, E. and Goode, J.G. (1977) *Anthropology of the city*, Englewood Cliffs, NJ: Prentice-Hall.

Edwards, R. and Caballero, C. (2008) 'What's in a name? An exploration of the significance of personal naming of "mixed" children for parents from different racial, ethnic and faith backgrounds', *The Sociological Review*, vol 56, issue 1, pp 39-60.

Faith, H. (1970) 'Black pearl precious little girl' [song released by Trojan Records; lyrics by Ian Levine, Irwin Levine, Phil Spector, Toni Wine (1969)].

Fraser, N. (1997) *Justice interruptus: Critical reflections on the 'postsocialist' condition*, New York: Routledge.

Gilroy, P. (2000) *There ain't black in the Union Jack*, London: Routledge.

Goffman, A. (2014) *On the run: Fugitive life in an American city*, Chicago: University of Chicago Press.

Gough, J., Eisenschitz, A. and Mcculoch, A. (2005) *Spaces of social exclusion*, London: Routledge.

Hanley, L. (2007) *Estates: An intimate history*, London: Granta.

Hall, S. (2000) *The multi-cultural question*, Milton Keynes: Open University Press.

Hastings, M. (2011) 'Years of liberal dogma have spawned a generation of amoral, un-educated, welfare dependent, brutalised youngsters', *Daily Mail*, 12 August.

Haylett, C. (2000) 'Modernisation, welfare and "third way" politics: limits to theorising in "thirds"?', *Transactions of the Institute of British Geographers*, vol 26, no 1, pp 43-56.

Haylett, C. (2001) 'Illegitimate subjects? Abject whites, neo-liberal modernisation and middle class multiculturalism', *Environment and Planning D: Society and Space*, vol 19, no 3, pp 351-70.

Haylett, C. (2003) *Culture, class and urban policy: Reconsidering inequality*, Oxford: Blackwell Publishing.

Hebidge D. (1979) *Subculture: The meaning of style*, London: Methuen.

Hebidge, D. (1983) '"Ska tissue": the rise and fall of two tone', in S. Davis and P. Simon (eds) *Reggae international*, London: Thames & Hudson.

Herrnstein, R.J. and Murray, C. (1994) *The bell curve: Intelligence and class structure in American life*, New York: Free Press.

Hewitt, R. (1986) *White talk, black talk: Inter-racial friendship and communication amongst adolescents*, Cambridge: Cambridge University Press.

Hewitt, R. (2005) The white backlash: The politics of multi-culturalism, Cambridge: Cambridge University Press.

Hill, A. (2007) 'Council estates spawn a new underclass', *The Observer*, 30 November.

Hirsch, D. (2013) *A minimum income for the UK in 2013*, York: Joseph Rowntree Foundation (www.jrf.org.uk/sites/files/jrf/income-living-standards-full.pdf).

Hoggart, R. (1959) *The uses of literacy*, London: Routledge.

hooks, b. (1984) *Feminist theory from margin to centre*, Boston, MA: South End Press.

hooks, b. (1991) *Yearning: Race, gender, and cultural politics*, London: Turnaround.

Jarratt, O. (2009) *The gifted one: Kirkland Laing through the eyes of others*, www.oliverjarratt.com.

Jensen, T. (2013) 'A summer of television poverty porn', The Sociological Imagination, 9 September (http://sociologicalimagination.org/archives/14013).

Johns, R. (2002) *St Ann's: Inner-city voices*, Warwick: Plowright Press.

Kendall, P. (2009) 'Broken Britain – can we fix it?', *The Telegraph*, 12 July (www.telegraph.co.uk/women/mother-tongue/5805205/Broken-Britain-can-we-fix-it.html).

Lawler, S. (2003) *Rules of engagement, habitus, power and resistance in feminism after Bourdieu*, Oxford: Blackwell Publishing.

Lawler, S. (2005) 'Disgusted subjects: the making of middle-class identities', *The Sociological Review*, vol 53, no 3, pp 429-46.

Lawler, S. (2008) *Identity: Sociological perspectives*, Cambridge: Polity.

Lewis, O. (1961) *The children of Sánchez: Autobiography of a Mexican family*, Harmondsworth: Penguin.

Lewis, O. (1966) *Four men – Living the revolution: Oral history of contemporary Cuba*, Urbana, IL: University of Illinois Press.

Levitas, R. (2005) *The inclusive society* (2nd edn), London: Macmillan.

Lister, R. (1996) *Charles Murray and the underclass: The developing debate commentaries*, London: IEA Health and Welfare Unit in association with *The Sunday Times*.

Lister, R. (2004) *Poverty*, Cambridge: Polity.

Littlejohn, R. (2014) 'Duggan was a gangster not Nelson Mandela', *Mail Online*, 10 January (http://dailym.ai/1tvagLR).

MacDonald, R., Shildrick, T., Webster, C. and Simpson, D. (2005) 'Growing up in poor neighbourhoods: the significance of class and place in the extended transitions of "socially excluded" young adults', *Sociology*, vol 39, no 5, December, pp 873-91.

Malone, C. (2008) 'Force low-life to work for a living', *News of the World*, 7 December, p 23.

SQW Consulting (2007) 'Tackling deprivation in Nottingham: Towards a 2020 roadmap. Discussion paper: challenges and priorities', SQW Consulting, May (www.nottinghaminsight.org.uk).

Nottingham City Council (2008) *Local government learning plan*, Nottingham: Nottingham City Council.

Nottingham City Council (2012) 'Child poverty: Nottingham City Joint Strategic Needs Assessment April 2012', www.nottinghaminsight.org.uk/insight/jsna/children/jsna-child-poverty.aspx

Nottingham City Council (nd) 'Budget consultation 2014/15' (www.nottinghamcity.gov.uk/yourcityyourservices).

Nottingham Evening Post (1958) 'Race riot in St Ann's', 17 August, online archive.

Ofsted (2012) *East Midlands regional report: Annual report 2012/13*, www.ofsted.gov.uk/local-authorities/nottingham

ONS (Office for National Statistics) (2007) *The English indices of deprivation 2007*, Communities and Local Government Publication, London: HMSO.

ONS (2010) *The English indices of deprivation 2010*, Communities and Local Government Publication, London: HMSO.

Orwell, G. (1962) *The road to Wigan Pier*, London: Penguin Books.

Owen, P. (2014) 'Mark Duggan lawfully killed, jury finds – as it happened', [blog] 8 January, www.theguardian.com/profile/paulowen

Phillips, M. (1998) 'Slums are not the problem: people are', *The Sunday Times*, 20 September.

Powell, E. (1968) Speech to Conservative Association meeting, Birmingham, 20 April, www.telegraph.co.uk/comment/3643823/Enoch-Powells-Rivers-of-Blood-speech.html

Reay D. (2008) 'Class out of place: the white middle classes and intersectionalities of class and "race" in urban state schooling in England', in L. Weis (ed) *The way class works*, New York: Routledge.

Reay, D. and Lucey, H. (2002) '"I don't really like it here but I don't want to be anywhere else": children and inner city council estates', *Antipode*, vol 32, issue 4, pp 410-28.

Rogaly, B. and Taylor, B. (2009) *Moving histories, of class and community*, London: Palgrave Macmillan.

Rowntree, B.S. and Lavers, G.R. (1951) *English life and leisure: A social study*, London: Longmans.

Savage, M., Scott, J. and Crompton, R. (2005) *Rethinking class, cultures, identities and lifestyle*, Basingstoke: Palgrave.

Sayer A. (2005) *The moral significance of class*, Cambridge: Blackwell.

Shildrick, T., MacDonald, R., Webster, C. and Garthwaite, K. (2012) *Poverty and insecurity: Life in low-pay, no-pay Britain*, Bristol: Policy Press.

Sibley D. (1995) *Geographies of exclusion: Society and difference in the West*, London: Routledge.

Sillitoe, A. (1958) *Saturday night and Sunday morning*, London: Harper Perennial.

Skeggs, B. (1997) *Formations of class and gender*, London: Sage.

Skeggs, B. (2004) *Class, self, culture*, London: Routledge.

Skeggs, B. (2005) 'The re-branding of class: propertising culture', in F. Devine, M. Savage, J. Scott and R. Crompton (eds) *Rethinking class: Culture, identities and lifestyle*, London: Palgrave.

Skeggs, B. (2009) 'Haunted by the spectre of judgement: respectability value and affect in class relations', in K. Sveinsson (ed) *Who cares about the white working class?*, London: RunnymedeTrust.

Skeggs, B. and Loveday, V. (2012) 'Struggles for value: value practices, injustice, judgment, affect and the idea of class', *The British Journal of Sociology*, vol 63, issue 3.

Slater, T. (2012) 'The myth of "Broken Britain": welfare reform and the production of ignorance, *Antipode*, 18 December.

Social Exclusion Task Force (2009) *Aspirations and attainment among young people in deprived communities*, London: Cabinet Office.

Strange, J. (2007) *Twentieth-century Britain: Economic, social and cultural change*, London: Pearson.

Townsend, P. (1954) 'Measuring poverty', *The British Journal of Sociology*, vol 5, no 2, June, pp 130-7.

Toynbee, P. (1998) 'The estate they're in', *The Guardian*, 15 September.

Tyler, I. (2013) *Revolting subjects: Social abjection and resistance in neoliberal Britain*, London: Zed Books.

Wacquant, L. (1994) 'The new urban colour line: the state and fate of the ghetto in post-Fordist America', in C. Calhoun (ed) *Social theory and the politics of identity*, Oxford: Blackwell, pp 232-4.

Wacquant, L. (2008) *Urban outcasts: A comparative sociology of advanced marginality*, Cambridge: Polity.

Wacquant, L. (2009) *Punishing the poor: The neo-liberal government of social insecurity*, London: Duke University Press.

Wacquant, L. (2010) 'Crafting the neoliberal state: workfare, prison fare and social insecurity', *Sociological Forum*, vol 25, no 2, pp 197-220.

Walkerdine, V., Lucey, H. and Melody, J. (2001) *Growing up girl: Psycho-social explorations of class and gender*, London: Palgrave.

Welshman, J. (2007) *Underclass: A history of the excluded, 1880-2000*, London: Continuum International Publishing.

West, E. (2009) 'How to create an underclass: stalk council estates handing out condoms', *The Telegraph*, 14 August.

Young, M. and Willmott, P. (2007 [1957]) *Family and kinship in East London*, London: Penguin.

Index